LIFE TO THE FULL

Rights and Social Justice in Australia

Published in 2007 by Connor Court Publishing Pty Ltd

© James Franklin and the authors of the individual chapters

All rights reserved

Connor Court Publishing Pty Ltd
PO BOX 1
BALLAN VIC 3342
Phone (03) 5368 2570
Fax (03) 5303 0960
anthony@connorcourt.com
www.connorcourt.com

ISBN: 978-1-921421-00-6

Front cover design by Ian James - ianjgd@bigpond.net.au

CONTENTS

Foreword - *Archbishop Philip Wilson*   i

A Note from the Publisher   iii

Introduction - *James Franklin*   1

Chapter 1 - The right to life
- *James Franklin*   15

Chapter 2 - The right to serve and worship God in public and private
- *John Sharpe*   19

Chapter 3 - The right to religious formation
- *Richard Rymarz*   27

Chapter 4 - The right to personal liberty under just law
- *Michael Casey*   33

Chapter 5 - The right to the equal protection of just law regardless of sex, nationality, colour or creed
- *Sam Gregg*   39

Chapter 6 - The right to freedom of expression
- *Damian Grace*   45

Chapter 7 - The right to choose and freely maintain a state of life, married or single, lay or religious
- *Marita Winters*   51

Chapter 8 - The right to education
- *Anthony Cleary*   57

Chapter 9 - The right to petition government for the redress of grievances
- *Paul Russell*   63

Chapter 10 - The right to a nationality
- *Andrew Hamilton*   69

Chapter 11 - The right to have access to the means of livelihood, by migration when necessary
- *Brenda Hubber*   75

Chapter 12 - The right of association and peaceful assembly
- *Michael Hogan*   81

Chapter 13 - The right to work and choose one's occupation
- *Ian Blandthorn*   87

Chapter 14 - The right to personal ownership, use and disposal of property subject to the right of others
- *Brian Coman*   93

Chapter 15 - The right to a living wage
- *Garrick Small*   99

Chapter 16 - The right to collective bargaining
- *Keith Harvey*   105

Chapter 17 - The right to associate by industries and professions to obtain economic justice
- *Henrik Jurisevic*   111

Chapter 18 - The right to assistance from society, if necessary from the State, in distress of persons or family
- *Catherine Althaus*   117

Afterword
- *James Franklin*   123

Contributors   125
Notes   129
Index   137

Foreword

Archbishop Philip Wilson

I am honoured to write this Foreword for the collection of essays being published under the title *Life to the Full*. It is easy to recommend the contributions provided by these authors. A distinguished and diverse group of authors. Their contributions express rich insights drawn from the Catholic tradition of Social Justice theory.

Some refer to Catholic Social justice teaching as the Church's best kept secret. I'm not so sure that this is accurate but I am sure that it deserves to be better known. This book will fit that purpose admirably.

My hope is that this book will provoke debate among those who consider a commitment to justice is an integral part of our Catholic Faith so that our commitment to justice can be refined and formed by the rich offerings presented here. I also hope that anyone who hasn't realised yet that a commitment to justice is required of all Catholics may be spurred into action by reading the book.

A NOTE FROM THE PUBLISHER

Christian Social teachings, like other aspects of the Church, are deeply polarised. On one side of the coin there are those who emphasise the life and bioethics issues such as abortion and euthanasia, while on the other side there are those who look at the justice issues such as refugees and the working conditions of workers. Both sides are keen to promote their own perspectives. What this amounts to is a problem wherein the Christian Social Teachings, in the Australian context, are not presented in their entirety. That is a great loss, as those teachings constitute a complete vision of society based on a coherent philosophy of rights.

In addressing this problem, we came across an important book written in the 1950s by Michael Fogarty entitled *Christian Democracy in Western Europe*. Although Fogarty was looking in that book at the European experience of the Christian Democratic Movement, he did explore in detail what was the total picture of the Social Teachings of the Christian Churches. Furthermore, in using the rights of the International Union of Social Studies drafted by the United States National Catholic Welfare Conference in 1947, he found 18 rights put forward as making up the total picture of the Christian Social Teachings. These 18 rights make up the chapters of this book.

Therefore, with these 18 chapters in mind, we set about finding 18 different people involved professionally in some ways with Christian Social Teachings, to each write a chapter on a particular right, keeping within a particular set of guidelines.

The first of these guidelines was to look at this right through the ten building blocks of Christian Social Teachings: the Human

Person, Human Life, Association, Participation, Preference for the Poor, Solidarity, Stewardship, Subsidiarity, Equality and the Common Good. Then the contributors were asked to state the principles involved in this right and the context on which these principles came about. Finally, they were to look at how it applies in the Australian context and what are the negatives that result when this principle is not applied as well as discussing how in an "everyday sense" a person can apply and promote the principles contained in these rights.

This work would not have come to fruition if it were not for the editor of the project, James Franklin, who not only guided the contributors, but also made certain that each chapter was in keeping with the guidelines.

The question now is: When one looks at the total picture, which political party in Australia best represents all 18 rights? Is it the Australian Labor Party, or the Greens? Is it the Liberal Party, the Nationals, the Australian Democrats or the resurgent Democratic Labor Party? This book does not seek to answer that question. Readers will make up their own minds. However, we hope that this book will serve as a checklist when it comes to looking at the policies and direction of those political movements in Australia.

Anthony Cappello,
Connor Court Publishing

Introduction

James Franklin

The late twentieth century saw two long-term trends in popular thinking about ethics. One was an increase in relativist opinions, with the "generation of the Sixties" spearheading a general libertarianism, an insistence on toleration of diverse moral views (for "Who is to say what is right? – it's only your opinion.") The other trend was an increasing insistence on rights – the gross violations of rights in the killing fields of the mid-century prompted immense efforts in defence of the "inalienable" rights of the victims of dictators, of oppressed peoples, of refugees. The obvious incompatibility of those ethical stances, one anti-objectivist, the other objectivist in the extreme, proved no obstacle to their both being held passionately, often by the same people.

The account of the Helsinki rights movement in Judt's magisterial history of late twentieth-century Europe, *Postwar*, demonstrates the power of rights as a moral and political weapon:

> In August 1975 the Helsinki Accords were unanimously approved and signed [between the major Eastern and Western countries]. On the face of things, the Soviet Union was the main beneficiary of the Accords ... it was agreed that the "participating states will respect each other's sovereign equality ... and "refrain from any intervention, direct or indirect, ... in the internal or external affairs ... of another participating State ..."

But also included ... was a list of rights not just of states, but of persons and peoples, grouped under Principle VII ("Respect for human rights and fundamental freedoms, including the freedom of thought, conscience, religion or belief") and VIII ("Equal rights and self-determination of peoples") Most of the political leaders who signed off on these clauses paid them little attention – on both sides of the Iron Curtain it was generally assumed that they were diplomatic window dressing, a sop to domestic opinion, and in any case unenforceable ...
It did not work out that way ... From this wordy and, it seemed, toothless list of rights and obligations was born the Helsinki Rights movement. Within a year of getting their long-awaited international conference agreement, Soviet leaders were faced with a growing and ultimately uncontrollable flowering of circles, clubs, networks, charters and individuals, all demanding "merely" that their governments stick to the letter of that same agreement ... Hoist on the petard of their own cynicism, Leonid Brezhnev and his colleagues had inadvertently opened a breach in their own defenses. Against all expectation, it was to prove mortal.[1]

There had been one major institution defending the objectivity of rights all along. It was the Catholic Church, which has always defended an objectivist "natural law" view of ethics in general and of rights in particular. On that view, ethics is not fundamentally about rules, or divine commands, or the greatest happiness of the greatest number, or habits ingrained by evolution and custom. It is about the irreducible worth of persons – the irreducible equal worth of persons – and what follows from that. Because a human being is of immense value, a human death is a tragedy. That is in contrast to the explosion of a lifeless galaxy, which is just a firework. So humans have a right to life and (to put the same thing from the point of view of others) murder is prohibited. Because humans have a particular nature, their rights and duties are of particular kinds. For example, because they are intellectual beings, knowledge is central to a full human life, which is to say they have a right to education. Because they are spiritual beings, they have a right to the free exercise of their religion. Because they have the responsibility to think autonomously about what is good for human life, they have the right not to be persecuted for their political or religious beliefs. And so on for the many other rights of individuals, which have come to be widely acknowledged as "human rights".

In thought on political and social organisation of society too, the late twentieth century saw developments that were in many ways a vindication of positions long held by the Catholic Church. Because humans are social beings with free will, they have a right to participation in the political and economic decisions that affect them. Leo XIII's 1891 encyclical *Rerum Novarum* laid out a vision of society between the extremes of state socialism and *laissez faire* capitalism. A society should consist of many organisations of different sizes and purposes cooperating in the context of an acceptance of moral rules. Families, trade unions, guilds, businesses, clubs and the state should pursue their own aims, respecting each other's spheres of action and cooperating to build a just society. A hundred years later, the Communist experiment in command economies had collapsed, and the form of "capitalism" successful in the West was so bound by safety regulations, compensation laws, truth-in-advertising legislation, powerful industry regulatory bodies and government inquiries as to be virtually unrecognisable as the *laissez faire* version of the nineteenth century. The "regulated capitalism" or "market socialism"[2] of the present day is much closer to Leo XIII's plan than to the socialist or capitalist rivals of his time.

Theory, unfortunately, has not kept pace with these developments, and much argument on the most abstract plane in economics and politics remains mired in unproductive wrangling between antique thoughtforms. On the one hand, state "socialism" as a top-down cure-all for injustices to the powerless is still advocated by those who have failed to answer criticisms of the overweening state's tendency to nationalise the means of oppression, as well as to impose inefficiency and stifle initiative and enterprise. From the other direction, polemic has been dominated by a Hayekian theory of capitalism that emphasises freedom at the expense of all other goods.

Despite its close correlation with actual historical developments, Catholic "social doctrine" has not made much impact outside the Church. It has not been widely studied and understood even within the Church. It has been generally seen, from a distance, as simultaneously platitudinous and necessarily false. It can seem platitudinous because it is moderate and balanced in its moral demands on economics and politics as well as close to the political reality we take for granted in the West. Like any position not sufficiently paradoxical to stand out, it risks the fate of Aristotle: "Aristotle's works are full of platitudes in much the same way as Shakespeare's *Hamlet* is full of quotations."[3] It seems false because *Realpolitik* and economic "forces" are presumed by self-styled hard-headed rationalists to be not subject to human command and hence beyond the reach of ethics.

Friedrich Hayek, the main theorist behind the moves towards "economic rationalism" and deregulation in the last thirty years, expresses the suspicions of many in his arguments on the "mirage of social justice". Only human actions can be just, he says, so states of affairs such as societal arrangements cannot be either just or unjust. For they are merely the unintended outcomes of the "self-organisation" of society through such means as market forces. The distribution of wealth resulting from "impersonal" market forces is not the result of the intention of any person or agency. Thinking it is would be to anthropomorphise "Society". Therefore, no one is to blame for that distribution and the concept of justice cannot apply to it.[4]

To the extent that an outcome is not foreseen or intended, to that extent it is indeed not subject to ethical judgement. But societies do not self-organise like eddies in turbulent fluids. Hayekians are captives of a certain simplistic model of self-organisation, the model derived from Adam Smith's "unseen hand". Such models of society have created a great deal of trouble. From Marx's fantasy of history as driven by inevitable conflicts of class interests to Dawkins' reduction of social interaction to the play of "selfish genes", attempts to explain society as the work of amoral agents hidden behind the scenes have had a ready audience. They play to the same market as books on the "Secret History of the Court of King So-and-So"[5] and the *Protocols of the Elders of Zion*, the market that revels in the exposure of dark forces holding the levers of power and the consequent relief of moral responsibility from those usually thought to have made the world as it is, ourselves.

But it is a matter of the most elementary observation that societies self-organise in a much more hierarchical and intentional way than fluids or ant colonies. They are much more like a game of a team sport. A game of football can look confused from a distance, and also from the point of a camera fixed to the ball. But it is not. The teams have coherence and are directed according to a conscious plan – though a plan that has to keep adjusting to unpredictable elements. The game as played is the outcome of interaction between the planned actions of the team and the cut and thrust of the ball and opposing play. So it is with economic and political ventures. The Great Pyramid, the East India Company, D-Day, Microsoft and for that matter the Catholic Church are great enterprises directed by minds. They are the outcomes of the ability of human institutions to achieve coordinated results by referring decisions to small groups who oversee a complex organisation directed to planned results. After the military, capitalist enterprises are among the most successful organisations in taking advantage of such possibilities; indeed, Weber points out that what distinguishes capitalism from mere buying and selling is its long-term planning with resources.[6] Businesses not only organise complex supply chains and market strategies individually, but cooperate to form Business Councils to lobby governments for subsidies and favours and to fund think-tanks promoting Hayekian ideas. The outcomes of those activities are both large-scale, intended and partially predictable in their outcomes. Therefore they are subject to the demands of justice. To the extent that the distribution of goods is a foreseeable result of those activities – and their point is, after all, to create and distribute certain goods – the distribution of goods is itself subject to the demands of justice. The extent of control or foreseeability of that distribution is not 100 per cent, outside a rigid command economy, nor should it be. But neither is it 0 per cent or close, as Hayek pretends. Hayek speaks as if justice would only be applicable to an all-powerful agent who would direct society and know with certainty the effects of its actions. But just as in the crime world there is no Mr Big but plenty of Mr Big Enoughs, so in society there are plenty of agents with considerable influence on the organisation of society and probable knowledge of the general tendency of the effects of their actions. Standards of justice are therefore applicable to their actions.

Hayek, indeed, admits that hierarchical self-organisation of society is possible. In fact, he spends much of his time warning how easy it is, constantly arguing that any restrictions on market forces will slip quickly into a totalitarianism that stifles freedom and enterprise. There is such a danger. But it is a danger only because of the innate tendencies of human societies to cede control up the line in order to get things done, a tendency that realises itself in many more partial ways than by dictatorship. When Hayek announces that the answer is "no" to both the questions:

1. "Whether within an economic order based on the market the concept of 'social justice' has any meaning or content whatever;

2. "Whether it is possible to preserve a market order while imposing upon it ... some pattern of remuneration based on the assessment of the performance or the needs of different individuals or groups by an authority possessing the power to enforce it,"[7]

the logical tension between the two "nos" is severe. It is like telling King Canute both that ordering the sea to go back is impossible and that doing so will dangerously distort the free flow of the tides.

The essential solution to the problem of how to impose social justice without falling into the evils of totalitarianism and a command economy is the one initiated by late medieval law and developed by Catholic social justice theory. Hayek himself praises the late medieval scholastics for their insight that "comparative prices arrived at without fraud, monopoly and violence was all that justice required."[8] True, but how does a freely "self-organising" society suppress fraud, monopoly and violence? Those constant temptations for the powerful will be major components of any spontaneous order, since an order is spontaneous precisely when those who have power exercise it without restraints. Fraud, monopoly and violence (and pollution[9], industrial accidents and the like) can only be suppressed – and thus prices be determined by economic reasons, that is as a result of free choices – by a strong legal system (of both criminal and commercial law), which can call on state sanctions to protect the rights of individuals. Indeed, the very existence of markets that violate rights can only be prevented by legal action – there are "market forces", in the sense of people prepared to pay, that would create free markets in slaves, child pornography, judicial decisions, liquidation of rivals, kidneys and babies if those sales were not illegal. Market forces do not have a meaning outside the system created by these legal restrictions: those restrictions on what may be bought and sold determine whether there can even be prices of such "products" as slaves, while regulations on work safety and pollution demand that businesses internalise their costs and hence include them in prices, instead of distributing them to hapless others. On the other hand, the legal system can create markets for ethical reasons, for example when copyright and patent law requires payment to the creators of intellectual property. Or the legal system can act to restrict the consequences of some free market decisions, in the way that bankruptcy law contains the downside risk of bad investment decisions by outlawing debt slavery. The law of contract, which declared contracts void in case of fraud or duress, was an early success in incorporating ethical requirements into the control of business.[10] Market "forces" have a very different meaning in a system not shaped by such an understanding and enforcement of fairness in contracts.

Only the state, acting in support of a legal system that is flexible about extending the protections of law, can accomplish those tasks. As John Paul II wrote in his encyclical on the hundredth anniversary of *Rerum Novarum*, "The State has the task of determining the juridical framework within which economic affairs are to be conducted, and thus of safeguarding the prerequisites of a free economy, which presumes a certain equality between the parties, such that one party would not be so powerful as practically to reduce the other to subservience," and "Economic activity, especially the activity of a market economy, cannot be conducted in an institutional, juridical or political vacuum. On the contrary, it presupposes sure guarantees of individual freedom and private property, as well as a stable currency and efficient public services. Hence the principal task of the State is to guarantee this security."[11]

Later developments in the same direction have been the strengthening in the twentieth century of compensation law to protect workers and consumers against unsafe work practices and products,[12] and more recently the strong regulation of matters of business ethics such as conflict of interest and insider trading. For products where the market cannot easily be informed because the quality of the offering takes a long time to become clear, such as life insurance, bank risk and some forms of education and medication, there is pressure for enforced inspection and publication of information; the pressure comes both from the public and from reputable firms concerned not to be undercut by "cowboys", and those industries are heavily regulated.[13] Again, market forces are created in the context of these legal and semi-legal restrictions. Regulated capitalism is successful because of the regulation, not despite it. The regulated and generally stable capitalism of the last few decades has delivered prosperity more reliably than the unrestrained capitalism of the Depression. And it is no accident that the world's most vibrant free enterprise society, the United States, is also the most litigious.

There are special difficulties with the regulation of the market in labour, where setting a minimum wage or imposing other industrial relations requirements on employment risks disadvantaging the unemployed. But interventions such as enforcing equal pay for equal work, non-discriminatory hiring practices and occupational health and safety standards have proved to be successful in the workplace without apparently retarding growth.

Mainstream economists, far from both Hayekian and socialist extremes, agree up to a point with these considerations, although they prefer to express themselves in ways that underplay the role of justice. They allow that the State may "support" the market in the "public good" situation (such as defence or health); the "externality" situation (as in taxing a polluter for the "quality of life" burden it imposes on others); the "merit good" situation (where it is accepted that goods such as education or social security should be provided even to those not prepared or unable to pay). The State may also "oversee" the market with watchdog bodies to enforce free competition and to correct information asymmetries by such means as publishing the results of restaurant kitchen inspections. Finally, the State may act macroeconomically by influencing interest rates to change the balances between growth, inflation and unemployment.[14] The State is also the only entity likely to coordinate interests over time intervals greater than those applicable to market mechanisms, for example in taking into account the rights of future generations in policy on environmental degradation and global warming. That is a very wide sphere of potential activity by the State, even taking into account warnings that the intervention should be as little as possible consistent with accomplishing the tasks. The economists normally prefer to justify these interventions in terms of "wants" such as the desire for defence, but the ethical language of "merit goods" and the like suggests that they really mean desires that are morally defensible.

None of those developments are totalitarian. They do not command prices or allocate goods. They simply restrict what can be done by businesses and others, in the interests of justice, before they can get to the point of setting prices by a market mechanism. Those developments have largely been accepted in practice, and the legal and compliance systems have enforced them (in Western countries) with a high degree of effectiveness. The cases of, for example, pollution in China and bribery in Russia remind us that this outcome is by no means a foregone conclusion.

If markets are structured ethically, Catholic social theory welcomes them.[15] Markets, when working well, are efficient at allocating effort and ensuring needs are met. They are not in themselves "materialistic" or based on any assumptions that humans are merely economic beings. They have the ability to fulfil demand, and what humans demand is up to them. If some people demand luxury consumables, there is a market in them; if others are prepared to pay for opera or charity services, that creates a market in those. If there is to be moral evaluation, it should bear on the choices people make, not on the existence of the markets to satisfy them. And it is markets that give people the opportunity to make their own choices on what is good for them and their dependants. It is especially in accordance with human dignity to be able to make that choice, using one's own information and responsible judgement.[16] Markets are also especially successful at encouraging innovation, which, in addition to better fulfilling needs, contributes to a richer human life for those who use their intelligence and hard work to imagine and implement a new process or product. Social justice is not only for the oppressed. Someone with a good idea also deserves justice, via a market that offers escape from the dead hand of red tape and vested interest by providing an opportunity for the idea to reach the public.

The other aspect of Leo XIII's vision that has proved successful in practice is the doctrine of the interplay of special-purpose societies. This too has medieval roots. The development of the notion of corporation allowed monasteries, universities, business companies and the like to be "legal personalities", owning and disposing of assets to pursue their special purposes. That allowed the development of an internal space relatively free from outside interference that allowed long-term innovative pursuits such as the universities' development of science and companies' overseas trading ventures.[17] The idea was expanded to politics with the separation of church and state and later the doctrine of separation of powers in Westminster constitutional democracies, in which legislative, executive and judicial arms of government have defined spheres of operation and agreed modes of interaction. As with the moulding of business relations by contract and compensation law, we can become so familiar with this organisation of society that we fail to perceive its uniqueness, but a comparison with a different way of doing things is instructive. Islamic societies do not admit a separation of church and state and do not have legally independent corporations, while the extreme example of monistic societal structure was Mao's China:

> The essence of totalitarianism is contained in the great helmsman's injunction to "put politics in command". This is not just Communist-Chinese baby-talk. What it means is this: that you are to take over every institution, whatever it may be, and empty out everything which distinguishes it from other institutions, and turn it into yet another loudspeaker for repeating "the general line". Destroy the specific institutional fabric of – a University, a trade union, a sporting body, a church – and give them all the same institutional content, viz. a political one. Contrapositively, the essence of resistance to

totalitarianism must consist in trying to maintain the specific institutional integrity of different institutions.[18]

Business companies are, indeed, among the special-purpose societies that can contribute to both general well-being and the human development of their members. In a properly-functioning marketplace, trust is essential to business,[19] while the necessity in business for long-term disciplined planning encourages certain virtues, such as prudence.[20]

Catholic theory does however take a positive view of the possibility of large-scale state action in support of the "common good", the collective goods like defence and the planning of health services that can only be realised in an organised society by centralised action. As Leo XIII put it, "it lies in the power of a ruler to benefit every class in the State, and amongst the rest to promote to the utmost the interests of the poor; and this in virtue of his office, and without being open to suspicion of undue interference – since it is the province of the commonwealth to serve the common good."[21] That is not to imply that the state should perform all the work. Privatised services or public-private partnerships may be the most efficient ways of providing, for example, telecommunications infrastructure or mass vaccination, but in that case attention moves to the service contracts and regulatory regimes under which the private contractors operate. The State must craft those carefully to ensure the providers secure their fee only by acting for the public good, and also that there is fair provision of essential services to those unable to pay full price.

More controversially, Catholic social theory approves of a limited degree of State action in support of redistribution of wealth. It does not aim at any particular distribution of wealth, for example an equal one, or advocate a "soak the rich" policy.[22] It does however rule out certain distributions of wealth as unjust, notably those in which the disadvantaged lack opportunities to work for their survival. For example, people disabled from birth are unlikely to make their way forward in a free marketplace, so justice requires that some of society's wealth should be redistributed to them. For the same reason, Catholic theory recommends some intervention in the labour market to ensure a minimum wage sufficient for a "condition of frugal comfort" for a worker and dependants (to use the phrase of Justice Higgins in the 1907 *Harvester* case, influenced by *Rerum Novarum*[23]). Economists rightly point to the problem that a minimum wage may disadvantage the unemployed by making it harder for them to gain employment, but it is impossible to believe that a healthy modern economy cannot easily provide the resources (through government action such as subsidies for apprenticeships, as well as wages directly from employers) to find useful work for all the able-bodied at a level of frugal comfort.

With the right to survival secured for all its members, the State can move to the protection of the other rights whose fulfilment is necessary for a complete human life, such as the rights to education, to participation in political decisions and to free expression.

It is clear then that the demand for social justice is neither meaningless nor platitudinous nor unrealistic. Immense efforts have been needed to implement the demands of justice and create a political, social and economic environment comparatively free from violence, intimidation, corruption, extremes of poverty, debt slavery, unsafe work practices, dangerous products, false advertising, insider trading, nepotism and all the other practices that accompany the naked and unrestrained abuse of power.

It is Catholic social justice theory that reveals how the order that protects us is founded on the worth of persons and consequent respect for their rights.

Chapter 1

THE RIGHT TO LIFE

James Franklin

When we are confronted with pictures of genocide victims dug up (e.g. of Srebrenica) we know "Those were people like us, and something terrible happened to them." Our emotional reaction gives us an immediate perception of the violation and destruction of something of immense value, a human life. It is gross violations of the right to life that most immediately force upon us a sense of the objective inviolability of human worth, which is the foundation of our knowledge of the objectivity of ethics in general and of rights in particular. To be sceptical about something as ethically basic as the terribleness of evil suffered by the victims of genocide would be not only wrong but an evil act against the victims of evil.[24]

To lack such emotions (as can happen for example with autistics) is to miss out on a crucial source of ethical understanding, and, as Jesus makes clear in the parable of the Good Samaritan, to fail to respond to a victim left for dead beside the road is to fail in our common humanity.

Christian thinking has always shown particular concern for the rights to life of those whom some more inhuman societies regarded as expendable, such as the physically or mentally disabled. As Pope John Paul II put it, "The starting point for every reflection on disability is rooted in the fundamental convictions of Christian anthropology: even when disabled persons are mentally impaired or when their sensory or intellectual capacity is damaged, they are fully human beings and possess the sacred and inalienable rights that belong to every human creature ... the more we move about in the dark and unknown areas of human reality, the better we understand that it is in the more difficult and disturbing situations that the dignity and grandeur of the human being emerges."[25] Human solidarity demands too that we remember those in mortal danger who are likely to be forgotten because "out of sight, out of mind"; they include political victims in dictators' gaols, infants in remote villages where there is no clean water, and babies soon to be born who do not always attract the medical assistance available to prematurely-born babies of the same age.

The only situations that can raise the serious possibility that a right to life should be set aside are those where the rights to life of different persons may conflict, as in self-defence when under immediate attack, or in a just war where failure to collectively defend civilisation risks disaster. Another traditional exception, capital punishment, is more doubtful. There may be extreme circumstances such as a city under siege where it is necessary to the survival of others, but it is hard to believe that there is any need for it in modern civilised society. "Today, as a consequence of the possibilities which the state has for effectively preventing crime, by rendering one who has committed an offence incapable of doing harm – without definitely taking away from him the possibility of redeeming himself – the cases in which the execution of the offender is an absolute necessity 'are very rare, if not practically nonexistent'."[26] There is, of course, no excuse for regarding heresy or apostasy as reasons for capital punishment, as has been believed by some religions in the past and present to the lasting discredit of religion in general.

The urgent necessity to preserve rights to life can justify interventions by the state and private persons that would not be advisable in more normal circumstances. The Catholic Church has been strong in its support of the rights of families against state intervention, but there are certain families in which children are at grave risk to their lives, and Leo XIII writes that "if within the precincts of the household there occur grave disturbance of mutual rights, public authority should intervene to force each party to yield to the other its proper due; for this is not to deprive citizens of their rights, but justly and properly to safeguard and strengthen them."[27] The same reasoning may justify interventions by states in other states where the right to life is being grossly violated by such acts as genocide or widespread torture; the excuse of "national sovereignty" has little weight beside the urgent demands of the victims (although the historical record of such interventions may suggest prudence in cases where there is a significant chance of making things worse).

Immediate threats to life are not the only situations where the right to life has implications for conduct. Constant attention to safety is demanded of individuals (for example, when driving cars), from those who design potentially dangerous products, equipment, buildings and services, and from both workers and employers at workplaces such as building sites. The work of those who increase lifespan, for example by medical practice and research, by military, police, security and judicial actions that suppress violence, by peace negotiations, or by work that raises safety standards and identifies and manages risks, is especially morally valuable because of its impact on the most basic of human rights.

The fundamental importance of the right to life means that it cannot be left as a matter of private morality. The political process cannot take a neutral stance to life, as if to say "Some people think the mentally ill (say) have a right to life, some don't, so in a pluralist society both sides must be free to act according to their beliefs". The very purpose of the State is, in the first instance, to protect life. "When he was told that the law could not legislate morality, Dr Martin Luther King, Jr, used to say that the law could not make people love their neighbors but it could stop their lynching them."[28] It has been a long and difficult process to create in the West a political order that by and large does protect the right to life of individuals from violence both from other individuals, from the state itself and from external threats. We owe a debt of gratitude to the many who contributed to it.

The implications of the right to life extend to questions of health, since poor health is, at least in rich and peaceful countries, the most immediate threat to life. The difference in life expectancy between mainstream and remote Aboriginal Australians is a sign of violations of the right to life, which indicates the need for inquiry and action as to the present causes of Aboriginal mortality such as violence, fetal alcohol syndrome, kidney disease and lack of educational and work opportunities.

In a world which contains sufficient resources to support all in moderate comfort and the means of transferring them, the lack of adequate food, water and health care for some is a scandal that implies violations of the right to life. That is taken up in other chapters.

There are questions about how the right to life applies at the beginning and end of life, where there are complex interactions among medical evidence, technological possibilities, intolerable conditions of life and compassion. There are other questions as to whether non-human animals have any worth and rights. Those are serious issues, but wondering about them should not shake our solid sense of the worth of persons. I have an accurate idea of what it would be like to be shot in an act of ethnic cleansing, simply because I am a human. We mourn the deaths of all those whose lives were cut short.

Chapter 2

THE RIGHT TO SERVE AND WORSHIP GOD IN PUBLIC AND PRIVATE

John Sharpe

We cannot be satisfied to be Christians at our devotions and merely secular reformers all the rest of the week, for there is one question that we need to ask ourselves every day and about whatever business. The Church has potentially to answer this question: to what purpose were we born. What is the end of Man? – T. S. Eliot, 1939

The right of which this short chapter treats is appropriately listed as second among those treated in this important anthology, for it is the foundation and root of those that follow. It might arguably have been made first – and chief – among the rights of this new Christian Social Manifesto; for even the right to life is itself ordered towards service to God, without which the very Purpose and Meaning of life are thwarted and vapid.

Taking as we do the Workers' Charter – *Rerum Novarum* of Pope Leo XIII – for magisterial foundation of Christian social teaching, we find that Leo deals with the right to serve and worship God in two paragraphs (§§40-1) where he demands that the State protect "the interests of [the] soul" of the workingman. The rationale offered for this is the fact that life on earth, "however good and desirable in itself, is not the final purpose for which man is created."

It is, rather, only a means to an end; the end, Leo, says, is the "attainment of truth" and the "love of goodness."[29] According to the essence of Catholic social thought, even these are themselves means to an end; as St Thomas puts it (*On Kingship*, §115), "... the beatitude of heaven is the end of that virtuous life which we live at present ..." This *eternal destiny* of man's soul is the essence, then, of that "human dignity" that, Leo reminds us in *Rerum Novarum*, "no man may outrage." Indeed the Pope goes so far as to say that regarding a matter that pertains to the pursuit of "that higher life which is the preparation of the eternal life of heaven," a man does not even have power over himself. To consent to any treatment "calculated to defeat the end and purpose of his being is beyond his right," for the rights in question are not, ultimately, man's, but rather they are God's.

As expected, among the specific rights and duties Leo enumerates under this heading is man's obligation – with its corresponding right – to worship God, keeping holy the Sabbath and other holy days through worship and "the cessation from work and labour." This narrow prescription we might take as one of the several specific rights implied in our general theme for this chapter: the right and duty of man to worship God, and especially to do so in private. This part of the problem is simple enough to frame, and, although it has been often violated throughout history, it is a right which no person of thought or feeling would on any grounds deny to another except in the rare case where a given religious practice infringes tangibly upon the rights of others to exercise the same right, or gravely contravenes the natural law, with ritual human sacrifice being a hackneyed but useful example.

The corollary right to worship God through all kinds of public observances and rituals is and always has been insisted upon with equal vigour by Catholic moralists, but the nature and origins of this right have not always been – and according to some are not even today – agreed upon. Catholics rightly insist upon their right to practise and manifest the Faith through specific religious acts, to include evangelisation, in public no less than in private. The same right, however, in an objective sense, was conceded to non-Catholic religions by the Vatican only recently in the history of the Church. Such a right is also insisted upon by the UN (in Article 18 of its Universal Declaration of Human Rights) – and uncontroversially so, especially for those who take the classically liberal foundations of modernity for granted. The question, however, of whether or not a society thoroughly Catholic (i.e., one in which a majority to the tune of 80 or 90 per cent of the population is Catholic) has the right, as a matter of religious "self-defence," to limit the public spread of religious ideas considered by the community to jeopardise the attachment of its citizens to the true and Catholic Faith still remains, though less practically relevant in modern times, important from a doctrinal and philosophical perspective.

In practice the distinction is of little significance, given the religious pluralism of modern nations, and the diversity of confession even in those countries of Europe and South America formerly, and "officially," Catholic. But those tempted to dismiss the question out of hand would do well to reflect on the essence of the Catholic position on society and social life. If, as St Thomas, Pope Leo and his successors, and numerous Catholic intellectuals ranging from the French Jacques Maritain to the American Ross J. S. Hoffman to the Irish Holy Ghost priest Fr Denis Fahey to Australia's own Archbishop Daniel Mannix have maintained, life in society is ultimately envisioned as a help to heaven, the question of a nation's hold on religious truth cannot be dismissed as a merely "personal" question of "freedom" based upon an *absolute* and *objective* recognition of a "right" to embrace a faith that, from a Catholic point of view, might jeopardise rather than enhance chances for eternal life.

Some modern thinkers have attempted such a dismissal, with a version of Decatur's cry along the lines of "my conscience right or wrong." Now Catholics have uncompromisingly affirmed that an individual's conscience is one of his "sovereign" possessions that should always and everywhere be free from coercion or pressure of any kind. But the degree to which public acts prompted by a private conscience, no matter how sincere or generally well-informed, are entitled to the same immunity from limitation is another question, and one at the centre of the political problem of maintaining an ordered society with a maximum of reasonable liberty. The Catholic solution to this problem has always been based upon the ordering of man's dignity and his sovereign, free conscience to his ultimate heavenly destiny – an ordering insisted upon with clarity and precision by Leo's Charter. Any attempt to envision that dignity in an absolute way, as the subject of *absolute* civil rights of whatever kind, will naturally run contrary, at least to some extent, to the Catholic position. The extensive debate on this issue as it relates specifically to "religious liberty" that took place before the beginning of the Second Vatican Council is evidence of its complexity. Even the Council declaration, *Dignitatis Humanae*, declares at the same time both that religious freedom should become a "civil right" and that the "traditional Catholic doctrine on the moral duty of men and societies toward the true religion" was left "untouched."[30]

The undisputed foundation of Christian social thought, and the rights derived from its premises, is the truth of Christ; as Dr Newman notes, that truth "is and must continue to be the ultimate objective criterion of action, whether individual or social."[31] The degree to which this fundamental premise is recognised in society, and the relationship between its degree and mode of recognition and the social conception of the right to religious freedom and expression, will be decisive for the moral quality and tenor of a society overall, not to mention its "Christian" character. Given the increasing moral and cultural degeneration of Western, liberal societies, the question of the public, social, and even political adherence of a society to certain fundamental truths beyond the merely "negative" ones sanctioned by the Enlightenment tradition takes on increasing importance.[32]

A final element of this right to "serve" God in public and in private goes beyond the simple question of public religious expression and worship, and considers the social framework itself as the forum that either aids the free pursuit of a virtuous and Christian life by members of society, or hinders that pursuit and thus infringes upon that freedom. A minimalist in the classical liberal tradition might interpret this in a purely negative way, meaning that there should be no laws, policies or specific government actions that actively impede the Christian's fulfilment of his duties as he conceives them with a reasonably formed conscience. This has never been the Catholic understanding, however. Social life should, if properly ordered, conduce to virtue, at least to the extent that conspicuous inducements to vice are prudently limited and even, in appropriate circumstances, legally suppressed. One need only think of the widespread immorality of film and television entertainment and advertising, the ready availability of pornography, contraceptives, abortion, and "no-fault" divorce, the growing movement towards the legal re-definition of the family from its traditional conception as a married man and woman with children, not to mention the stacking of the economic deck more and more against the middle class and small family farmer and business owner, to take stock of the wide field of action wherein the Catholic legislator or politician might busy himself with pursuing a social atmosphere that would put fewer obstacles in the way of citizens seeking to live virtuous lives.

Evidence for this argument is plentiful in Catholic sociological scholarship; I offer just one example of the way it has been expressed by Catholic thinkers. According to Dr Goetz Briefs, a Georgetown University sociologist addressing a National Catholic Rural Life Conference in American, ca. 1935:

> [O]ur social and economic institutions must be built in such a way that ... the average Christian can find his way to his ultimate salvation without struggling heroically and with the grace of a selected saint against the daily things tempting him toward unnatural and graceless life ...

Considered from this point of view, a Christian social manifesto must grapple not only with fundamental "religious" rights, but with the many social qualities and characteristics, even on the natural and secular plane, necessary for a society to aid Catholics and Christians in the fulfilment of moral duties and in the pursuit of virtue. "[T]he greatest contribution the Catholic Church has to offer to the present generation," Dr Briefs continued,

> [and] to the salvation of the occidental world lies here, in restoring *natura hominis* and *societatis* in order that the grace of God, this great historical causality, can work its way to the salvation of man and to the welfare of our modern world.[33]

From this principle does all of Christian social teaching flow, as well as its numerous corollary ideas, such as the indirect power of the Church over temporal affairs, the role of the Catholic laity in Christian social action, the need for private ownership of productive property by heads of families, and the subordination of economic life to right reason and morality.

A final word highlighting the essential connection between the narrow right to freedom of worship and the wider notion of that "Christianisation" of society necessary for Christians properly to enjoy the freedom to serve God in all aspects of public and private life, is left to the great American-turned-Englishman T. S. Eliot, who was himself a perceptive social critic and essayist as well as a widely respected poet and man of letters. As early as 1938 he warned against construing freedom of religion for Christians in an overly narrow fashion, in a work in which he termed "intolerable" the predicament of Christians attempting to live Christian lives in non-Christian surroundings. "We must abandon," he wrote,

> the notion that the Christian should be content with freedom of *cultus*, and with suffering no worldly disabilities on account of his faith ... [T]he Christian can be satisfied with nothing less than a Christian organization of society – which is not the same thing

as a society consisting exclusively of devout Christians. It would be a society in which the natural end of man – virtue and well-being in community – is acknowledged for all, and the supernatural end – beatitude – for those who have the eyes to see it.[34]

It is with the vision of Pope Leo XIII and in his spirit that the foregoing considerations have been offered, for it is only by returning to first principles that we may hope to restore to our beleaguered Western civilisation that vitality and energy which was its characteristic in former and better days: "When a society is perishing, the wholesome advice to give to those who would restore it is to call it to the principles from which it sprang ..."

Chapter 3

THE RIGHT TO RELIGIOUS FORMATION

Richard Rymarz

Formation, in Catholic circles, has long had a connotation of something that is restricted to the clergy and those in religious life. Many religious congregations, for example, have specified periods of formation prior to ordination or profession. This can involve quite lengthy amounts of time and involve highly structured activities. In a contemporary interpretation, however, formation is something which applies to all as a manifestation of the priesthood of all believers. It is not uncommon in the Church today, for example, to see many groups arising which promote a distinctly non-clerical or religious approach to formation. Sanctity is seen as something which is within the reach of all and it is understood that involvement in the world as opposed to the cloister does not disqualify one from the serious cultivation of religious beliefs and practices. Moreover these can be developed alongside a professional or family life.

An important dimension of the Church's understanding of human dignity moves beyond the right to profess religious beliefs to the more elusive goal of the right to nurture and cultivate these. For the sake of clarity formation, in this essay, will be discussed using Catholicism as a template but the idea of a right to religious formation can be applied to all believers and even to those who hold to philosophical positions that have religious overtones. The right to formation would apply to any religious group for example but it is not absolute and does have limits. If a group saw formation as an opportunity to direct people towards acts of violence against the common good then this should not be tolerated.

One of the great themes of the Second Vatican Council was the right to religious liberty. This was set out in, principally, the Decree on Ecumenism – *Unitatis Redintegratio* – but also alluded to in the great conciliar constitutions *Lumen Gentium* and *Gaudium et Spes*. This somewhat controversial but classical theme, in as much as it represented a new emphasis in Catholic teaching, was prominently discussed in the aftermath of the Council where it was a much anticipated teaching. A lesser known but emerging aspect of contemporary Catholic social teaching, without a long history of development and discussion, is the right to religious formation. This is nonetheless a clear implication of the Council's stress on the irreplaceable role of the laity as the Church's face to the world and a response to fresh realities which are especially prevalent in the developed world. Part of the emerging social context, which has led to a greater awareness of the importance of formation, is a new situation where the Church sits in a milieu where the characteristic interaction between Church and State is increasingly seen as one of disjuncture and not of close interaction be it hostile or otherwise. Classical Catholic social thinking on Church–State relations in many countries needs to be more aware of the more extensive implications that follow on from the right to religious liberty.

Formation can be best understood as growth in faith. It presupposes some preexisting connection to an active faith community and an acceptance, in some form, of the salvific reality of the Christian message. In this way it can be distinguished from evangelisation, which has as its goal the proclamation of the gospel to those who have not heard it. In post-industrial Western societies such as Australia many people have some affinity with the Christian story. They may have attended Church schools or had religious parents or grandparents. They may mark special occasions such as Christmas with a religious ambience. They are not being denied a right to religious liberty. They are not, properly speaking, in need of evangelisation although the concept of New Evangelisation, popularised by Pope John Paul II, where people are reintroduced to the gospel message in lands that have a long historical Christian association, could be applied to them.

The Church has sought to highlight in more recent times the need for individuals to cultivate a deeper sense of belonging to their religious communities as manifested by a closer relationship with Jesus as evidenced by prayer, sacramental life and personal conduct, especially as in terms of developing a strong social conscience. Formation here, rightly understood, is a life-long process – one can always imagine a situation where a person's relationship with Jesus could be strengthened. Formation is also then a deeply personal endeavour. On one level formation will follow an individual's path based on the interests, strengths and situation of the person. Formation is not a one-size-fits-all process but needs to recognise individual differences. Consider the life situation of a child about to receive their first communion, a young adult contemplating marriage or a worker approaching retirement. Each person is at a different stage of their life journey and each has specific formation needs. We see here a clear manifestation of the conciliar emphasis on the duty of each person to strive for personal holiness. This is not a precursor of an individualistic atomised faith but rather recognition that many of the social and cultural factors which assisted religious belief and observance in earlier times are no longer present in countries such as Australia. In such an environment the personal commitment of the believer to cultivating the gift of faith takes on greater significance.

A term used to describe the nurturing process of formation is catechesis. In his Apostolic Exhortation *Catechesi Tradendae*, published in 1979, Pope John Paul II spells out the right of believers to catechesis: "from the viewpoint of human rights, every human being has the right to seek religious truth and adhere to it freely, that is to say, 'without coercion on the part of individuals or of social groups and any human power'."

Catechesis is not to be confused with catechetics, which is a style of didactic pedagogy. Catechesis is often described as a dialogue between believers and this captures a critical point about formation, that at its heart is based on human relationships. The forum for catechesis, therefore, is the faith community. If we see formation as a strengthening of the fundamental Christological relationship then there are a variety of ways that this can be achieved and all of these need to be recognised and promoted. The premier place of formation is not an institution such as the school or university. As spelled out by Pope John Paul II in *CathechesiTradendae* and elsewhere, educational agencies have a role to play in catechesis but their focus is, broadly speaking, on growth in knowledge. The notion of the school as a faith community has become more problematic. In many contemporary Catholic schools, for example, one cannot make easy assumptions about the religious commitment of the students and staff. Students come from a variety of backgrounds, including a growing proportion from non-Catholic background, and whilst schools have a role to play in catechesis the primary locus of religious formation lies elsewhere. To give an example, a school can teach students about a topic such as reconciliation. It can encourage students to receive the sacrament and provide opportunities by coordinating visits by priests. The school alone cannot, however, engender a love of the sacrament and its frequent reception. This attitude is fostered only in some type of faith community where mentoring and nurturing is given. For most people, certainly adolescents, this community is the family. If formation is not occurring in the home then schools and other institutions cannot be expected to make up the deficiency although many make splendid efforts in this regard. The current debate about the role of Catholic schools in faith formation is an important and timely one but it needs to recognise that any efforts the Catholic school makes are secondary and complementary to the role of the primary faith community. If the student is not part of such a primary faith community then ways of overcoming this can be investigated but it is not a simple or straightforward issue. The right to religious formation is one reason that the family is given such a prominent place in contemporary Catholic social thought. Ways to strengthen the formative role of the family are therefore given high priority in contemporary Catholic social thought. This is not only because the family is a bulwark against many social evils but it also provides the positive environment needed to sponsor formation.

Catechesis is also a broad term. It is not confined to learning about something. It involves all the believer does to strengthen their bond with Christ. Individuals have a right, therefore, to become involved in activities which allows for this to occur, whether in private or public fora. Part of a formative process, especially for young people, is the right to associate with others in a public display of religious belief and affiliation. This is formative in the sense that it gives to individuals a greater sense of plausibility as their religious beliefs can be seen as overlapping with those of others that religious belief is not marginal and defunct. Another example of the right to religious formation involves free access to multimedia by religious agencies. These modes of communication are especially important to young people who are difficult to reach using conventional means of mass communication such as the printed media.

Chapter 4

THE RIGHT TO PERSONAL LIBERTY UNDER JUST LAW

Michael Casey

"The right to personal liberty under just law" is not a native phrase of the Australian vernacular. Australians instead speak simply of freedom, and in doing so take a number of things for granted.

First, the word *freedom* is not spelt with a capital letter. It is not treated as the meaning of life and the purpose of history. Nor is it regarded as an absolute. For Australians, freedom is no illusion and its reality is not in doubt, but it does not exist by itself or have supremacy over all other values. The ethos of a fair go and a culture of egalitarianism continue to condition the understanding of how freedom works and what it means. Australians are in no sense fatalistic and have always distinguished themselves by the imaginative practicality with which they create opportunities, overcome obstacles and expand horizons. At the same time, a sharp and unsentimental awareness of how circumstances can make life a real battle for some people prevents them from believing in the limitlessness of possibility. This keeps the idea of freedom well-grounded in the reality of human experience.

Second, no illusions are harboured about the law. While this is no guarantee of its capacity to dispense justice, it does tend to make it more or less unproblematic. The existence of political corruption and the abuse of law at the beginnings of European settlement are often over-stated, but both have made sporadic and significant appearances throughout Australian history. This has reinforced a natural scepticism of authority and made Australians resistant to efforts to obscure or mystify the workings of power. It has also given them a pragmatic attitude to the creation and administration of the law. Laws are made for a particular purpose and those purposes should be pursued fairly. Where the law ceases to be fair it should be changed. The success or failure of a law is assessed on its results, and the same criterion applies to the judges and the courts. The courts are respected in Australia not only because of their long record of probity, but also because of the general fairness of their verdicts. It is outcomes Australians look to, not institutions. The veneration of the constitution in the United States and its cult of the Supreme Court is unimaginable in Australia.

As in every constellation of human affairs there is light and shadow here. Freedom for Australians effectively means no more than personal liberty under just law. Freedom has no meaning to them as a project for creating new worlds. It means being left in peace to order one's own affairs as one sees fit, and to take advantage of the opportunities of Australian life as one chooses. This takes place within certain parameters, one source of which is the law, and it is assumed that most laws most of the time are just, or close enough to it. This prosaic and pragmatic approach to the great themes of modern society and politics is sometimes an embarrassment to intellectuals and occasionally a cause of bitterness and derision for some in other professions who take politics too seriously. In this they fail to appreciate the genius of the Australian achievement. Australia became a nation while Europe was incubating the "great politics" which would take modernity beyond all restraint. Without great politics Australia built a society which people in almost every preceding age would look upon as a type of utopia. Politics based on romanticism or rarefied principle has flooded the world with blood, but Australians seemed to know from the beginning what others are still learning through suffering: that poetry and projects for salvation do not belong in politics.

None of this means that principle and idealism do not have a place in Australian life or have not played a part in Australian history.

Nor does it mean that the promises of radical ideologies have never exercised an appeal. But these forces have inevitably come up against the limits set by the peculiar type of realism that characterises the Australian outlook. This has certainly been for good but it has also worked to ill. Australia is not, of course, a utopia, and serious problems and injustices continue to exist. Some of these arise precisely from Australians' scepticism about appeals to high principle over lived existence, and their susceptibility to go for what works and seems fair over what are perceived to be remote or abstract truths. Abortion is a typical example. Australians do not particularly like abortion and they understand what it entails. But they want it to be available as a last resort for women who decide they need it. So, leaving someone to sort this problem out for herself, especially when she is the one facing it most immediately, seems the fairest thing to do, even though it results in unjust law and the destruction of innocent life.

There is confusion and incoherence throughout the Western world about the meaning of freedom and how far the right to personal liberty extends. Australia shares in this in its own particular way. But it also has some particular advantages when it comes to the task of recovering what George Weigel has called "a better concept of freedom". Foremost among them is a strong sense that freedom has a purpose which in some way is bound up with the good of others.

In Catholic moral philosophy and social teaching, freedom is one of the markers of the divine origins and the "sublime dignity" of every human being. Respecting the right to exercise freedom and the right to freely take responsibility for ourselves and others is part of what respecting human dignity means. The right to personal liberty also entails the right of the individual to pursue his own vocation, to profess his religious convictions, and to follow his political and cultural ideas. A further important aspect of respect for freedom and personal liberty is respecting the right of the individual to resist anything that is morally negative or destructive, and to distance himself from anything that hinders personal, family or social growth. Personal liberty operates within limits imposed by the common good and the rule of law, which also ensure its protection.

Freedom is not an abstraction. It is lived in the real world among real people. This means it is always exercised in some sort of relationship to others. Pope John Paul II warned against the idea of freedom as "radical assertion of self *against* others". Treating freedom as complete and unlimited personal autonomy denies the relational nature which provides its meaning and purpose. It also leads to a practice of freedom which ultimately undermines it. If freedom is only for the good of the individual and regard for others only an optional extra, life becomes an unending contest of wills in which the strongest takes all. Freedom is cancelled out in a struggle for domination, a struggle to make one's own will prevail. For the most part the consequences of this are felt in the personal realm, in the way relationships are blighted and friendships stunted by the experience of exploitation and the fear of being vulnerable. Eventually, this may or may not translate into problems of political domination. In any case, freedom as the assertion of self against others is not a sustainable foundation for democracy or any form of life in common.

Each individual exists as someone unique and unrepeatable. The capacity for self-understanding, self-determination and self-possession which sets us apart from the animal world can only be fully realised by accepting our dependence on others when we are weak and our responsibility for others when we are strong. No human being can escape dependence and responsibility, although the confrontation with them can be resisted. This resistance explains a deal of modern secular culture and its adamant insistence on freedom as the supremacy of the individual over all personal, communal and civic attachments. In this vision, freedom means that we are only bound to others to the extent that we choose to be, and are always free to walk away regardless of who might need us.

Against this the Church offers an idea of the human person as a unity of reason, freedom and love. Human life and society flourish when these three things are held together. When this unity is fragmented, human life and society begin to fragment as well. Freedom is not diminished by being joined to love and reason. Without them, freedom degenerates into an empty supremacy, but with them it becomes full of purpose and meaning. It ceases to be an abstract state or condition, and becomes something dynamic, with a clear direction. That direction is away from ourselves and towards others. Instinctively we want freedom to enrich us. Counter-intuitively perhaps, we find these riches in giving, in service to others. Treating freedom as something to be taken and hoarded leads only to bankruptcy.

The right to personal liberty under just law takes each of us to the question of how we are to live our freedom in relation to others. In answering, we can choose lonely supremacy or mutual dependence. It is a mistake to assume that the right choice will always be made automatically. If we want Australia to continue to be a fair and decent society we need to make sure that the reasons for choosing the better concept of freedom are renewed and replenished in each generation.

Chapter 5

THE RIGHT TO EQUAL PROTECTION OF JUST LAW REGARDLESS OF SEX, NATIONALITY, COLOUR OR CREED

Sam Gregg

Today the idea that all individuals are entitled to equal protection by just laws is a moral and legal concept taken for granted in most of the West. Yet despite the fact that this idea is firmly rooted in the genius of the West's Judaeo-Christian civilisation and has been a consistent feature of most Western jurisdictions for centuries, its full implementation has taken much longer.

As recently as 1900, whole categories of people did not enjoy equal protection of just law, precisely because of factors such as their sex or skin colour. In countries ranging from South Africa to Australia, those who did not come from European backgrounds were unjustly discriminated against by government legislation, not to mention constitutional and common law.

Australian Aboriginals, for instance, were not accorded the right to vote and therefore participate in Australian public life to the same extent as other Australians, on the unjust basis that they were Aboriginal. They did not gain the full privileges associated with citizenship until a series of Commonwealth and state laws were passed from 1948 onwards.

Equal protection by law is based on the premise that all people should be equal before the law. This means that when a law is made, every person subject to that law must be treated equally. Thus when a law is applied or enforced, there should be no discrimination or differentiation in its application or enforcement, except on a reasonable and justifiable basis.

The important qualification of "reasonable and justifiable basis" reflects the fact that not all forms of legal discrimination are unjust. There are good reasons, for example, why we do not issue gun licenses to children. This does not mean that children are not owed equal respect as persons. But the child may be legitimately denied a shooting license because a child-person *is* different from an adult-person with respect to the degree of responsibility they can be reasonably expected to exercise vis-à-vis guns. In this instance, discrimination is not unjust. It is, in fact, an act of reasonable and just discrimination.

In the pre-Christian ancient world, the law held there were two categories of human beings: citizens and slaves. They were therefore treated differently by the law. This was justified on the grounds that before they were human beings, slaves were their masters' property. Like any other piece of property, they could be treated by their owners in ways forbidden by the laws ordering relationships between citizens. Slaves beaten by their citizen-owners generally had no recourse to the law for protection. By contrast, citizens beaten by fellow-citizens could immediately apply for legal redress.

Over the centuries, it became apparent that these and similar laws and their applications violated the principle of equal protection by just law. The centuries-old struggle against slavery sparked by Christianity's insistence upon the equal dignity of every human person gradually resulted in the abolition of laws permitting slavery.

When Australia was first permanently settled by Europeans, formal participation in colonial public life (most notably through voting or eligibility to hold public office) was initially limited to male property-owners without a criminal record. Over time, these rights were extended to women and those owning little or no property.

The rationale underlying these changes was the realisation that it was unreasonable and therefore unjust for the law to treat women and non-property owners differently when it came to voting or eligibility to hold public office. Laws permitting such discrimination were understood as unjust and therefore changed so that they conformed to the requirements of reason and justice.

This is not to suggest that progress in entrenching the idea of equal protection by just law has not suffered periodic setbacks at different times and places. The Nuremberg race laws implemented by Germany's National Socialist dictatorship removed the protection of law from German Jews by effectively declaring Jews to be non-citizens and promoting policies that undermined the ability to Jews to own and use property, marry, and participate in public life. Likewise the Nazi euthanasia program was premised on the regime's removal of the law's protection from the mentally and physically disabled. In a similar manner, the passing of legislation or court judgments throughout the post-war West, including Australia, permitting the intentional abortion of unborn children may be understood as undermining the equal protection from arbitrary killing accorded by law to all innocent human beings.

Since 1945, two debates through the West have emerged concerning equal protection by just law. The first concerns whether the principle is primarily "negative", in the sense that the law simply adjudicates alleged instances of people not being treated equally by the law without reasonable cause, or whether equal protection means that the law may be used as a means to promote groups allegedly suffering from unjust discrimination.

It is one thing for a court to rule that it is unjust for public officials or private citizens to prevent women or non-whites from voting. It is, however, quite another matter for a court or government to claim equal protection means that public and private organisations ought to be legally compelled to "positively discriminate" in favour of certain groups in order to diminish apparent social and economic disadvantages. This is at the heart of arguments concerning, for example, affirmative action laws that compel public and private associations to hire quotas of certain categories of people (e.g., women, non-whites, the elderly etc). No matter how well-intended, such programs, ordinances, and laws violate the principle of equal protection by just law insofar as they require unjust legal discrimination against qualified people who do not fall into such categories.

This leads us to the second post-war debate about equal protection by law. This concerns the meaning of "just law." From the time of the Greek philosopher Aristotle, it was understood that if a law was to be just, it had to be made by a legitimate public authority according to established and just principles governing the making and amending of laws, and could not contradict pre-existing laws without appropriate amendments being made to such laws. Conformity with established procedures for making laws was, however, only part of the criteria for determining whether a law was just. It was also understood that if a law was to be just, it could not contradict what was called the "natural law." In short, a man-made law was not true law if it violated the moral law revealed to human beings through the correct use of their reason. This was powerfully and eloquently expressed by Pope Pius XI in his 1937 anti-Nazi encyclical letter, *Mit Brennender Sorge*:

> We are especially referring to what is called the natural law, written by the Creator's hand on the tablet of the heart (Romans 2:14) and which reason, not blinded by sin or passion, can easily read. It is in the light of the commands of this natural law, that all positive law, whoever be the lawgiver, can be gauged in its moral content, and hence, in the authority it wields over conscience. Human laws in flagrant contradiction with the natural law are vitiated with a taint which no force, no power can mend. (*MBS* no. 30)

This constituted a direct assault on the Nazi idea that a law's justice was derived from the simple fact that it has been made by a legitimate public authority. But more generally it constituted a critique of "positivism" - the belief that law is whatever the people, courts or rulers want it to be, regardless of what natural law and reason tells us. In this context, a law's justice no longer depends upon whether it accords with the demands of natural reason, but rather because it has received majority approval from a legislature or court.

A timeless issue concerning equal protection of just law concerns the manner in which those people living in a country of which they are not a citizen (e.g., permanent residents, refugees etc) generally do not enjoy the same protections of just law accorded to citizens. They generally cannot, for example, vote despite the fact that they may pay taxes in that country. In some instances, their choice of where to live or their ability to seek employment does not receive the same protection from the law of their host country compared to that accorded to citizens.

There is no one catch-all principle or rule capable of resolving each and every one of these questions. To take the case of immigrants: it is surely reasonable for the law to treat differently those who enter a foreign country legally and who have fulfilled all the often-onerous requirements of obtaining permission to live and work permanently in that country, compared to someone who has entered the same country by violating its laws concerning how and when people may enter that country.

But even in the case of legal immigrants, there is a reasonable case for denying them the right to vote in the elections of their host country until they decide that they wish to become citizens of that country. Citizenship implies a willingness to assume the duties of a citizen and a commitment to the host country that is not forthcoming from a person who decides to retain the status of permanent resident and therefore citizenship of another country.

Likewise, the fact that an illegal immigrant entered a country in violation of its laws is not a justification for denying that person basic rights such as protection from arbitrary killing or theft of their private possessions. These protections are accorded to people regardless of their citizenship precisely because they are not associated with the rights of citizenship per se, and instead are derived from the respect these people are owed simply by virtue of being human beings.

The complexity of these cases illustrates that Australians must constantly ask ourselves whether a proposal that claims to extend the equal protection of each individual by just law is consistent with the principles underlining this idea, or if the proposal actually undermines equal protection by just law. History is replete with backward steps in the extension of this idea in the name of progress or a desire to diminish discrimination. It would be a tragedy if just law in Australia was progressively eroded by false applications of a principle that testifies to the truth of every human being's equal worth precisely as a human being.

Chapter 6

THE RIGHT TO FREEDOM OF EXPRESSION

Damian Grace

The affirmation of human freedom by the Church goes back to its origins, but it is an ambivalent affirmation, tempered by the knowledge that while freedom is a condition for virtue, it can also licence vice.[35] The right to free speech is proclaimed in Article 20 of the Universal Declaration of Human Rights. It receives constitutional protection in some countries, most famously in the United States. Although the Australian Constitution does not explicitly mention this right, the High Court has found an implied constitutional protection of free speech.[36] The Catholic Church is not usually numbered among the strong defenders of free expression. Quite the contrary: Protestant and Enlightenment thinkers have often defined their demands for freedom against the strictures of the Church. The case of Galileo and the Index of books Catholics were forbidden to read are but two polemical clichés among many centuries of examples of repression in the name of truth. Indeed, recognition of this moved Pope John Paul II to apologise, among other things, for the Church's conduct in the Galileo matter. So, what is the Church's current position on freedom of expression?

The Catholic Church is not a debating society. Its purpose is to spread the Gospel of Jesus Christ, not to promote philosophical discussion. The Church cannot honestly adhere to its mission while publicly encouraging doubt about it. It teaches unambiguously that the Gospel proclaims truth. The Church also proclaims a special role for itself in safeguarding faith and morals. It would be absurd for it to teach at the same time that its doctrines and role were open questions. Historically, the Church has tried to safeguard the faith by actively suppressing open discussion. Yet when force was used on Christ's behalf at Gethsemane, and the high priest's servant lost his ear, Jesus healed the injured man and reproved his disciples (Luke 22:51; John 18). Jesus did not rely on the sword; nor should the Church. Modern regimes have specialised in denying free expression, and the Church has had to deal with this: Pius XI's anti-Nazi encyclical, *Mit Brennender Sorge* of 1937, was distributed clandestinely in Germany because there was no possibility of issuing it through normal channels. Now that its voice is challenged in liberal democracies, the Church runs the risk of appearing selective in its defence of free expression. More positively, Pope John Paul II has affirmed not only that freedom of expression is necessary to its mission, but also that this and other freedoms derive from that mission.[37]

In 1888, three years before he issued his landmark encyclical, *Rerum Novarum*, Pope Leo XIII published a less well known encyclical, *Libertas* or *Liberty*, in which he cautioned that freedom brings with it large responsibilities that condition its proper use. Truth and error do not have equal rights and so the notion of a right to be in error and to spread that error cannot be a positive right.[38] This has been the Church's long-standing view of freedom, and has brought it frequently into opposition with those who are reluctant to acknowledge any grounds for abridging free expression. Leo's encyclical is echoed strongly in John Paul II's *Veritatis Splendor* (1993).[39] In modern Australia, the traditional teaching of the Church on freedom of expression is difficult to understand because it is at variance with many prevalent political and moral assumptions. In our society, it is difficult to harmonise liberal assumptions with religious belief.[40] Although some writers believe that the dignity of the individual unifies liberal and Catholic doctrines of freedom,[41] this is not immediately obvious. For liberals, the freedom of the individual is paramount, especially where this is the freedom to decide what is right and wrong. The maxim often invoked is that misattributed to the eighteenth-century French thinker Voltaire: "I disapprove of what you say, but I will defend to the death your right to say it." (Voltaire would have done no such thing.) For the Church, the word of God and His plan of salvation trump all political and social values and the individual is not free in the liberal sense to decide right and wrong.[42] None of this denies the importance of conscience in guiding conduct.[43]

The right to freedom of expression is a fundamental right but it is neither inalienable nor unlimited. The common good or other sufficient reasons can limit this right, and the law recognises this. For example, in time of war, freedom of expression might be limited in the interests of national security. Again, one is not permitted to shout "fire" in a crowded theatre. The good of others limits the liberty of expression. This liberty is not on an equal footing with absolute rights, such as a right not to be unjustly killed. In encyclicals from Leo XIII to John Paul II, the right of free expression is conditional on the nature of what is expressed: freedom depends on truth. Without truth, freedom turns into arbitrariness and thus extinguishes itself.[44] Benedict XVI has emphasised the moral responsibility that goes with liberty of expression, namely respect for "the fundamental dignity of the person and of human groups" and their religious beliefs.[45] This emphasis on responsibility does not in any way diminish the importance of the right to free expression for the proper participation of citizens in the social and political life of their communities.[46]

The Church's teaching, however, goes beyond this to the positive encouragement of people to use their freedom to express the truth and to correct error. There is a common assumption in liberal democracies, such as Australia, that everyone is entitled to their own opinion, that there can be no such thing as a "wrong" opinion, and that toleration requires a kind of passive acceptance of difference. This attitude can encourage silence and thereby assist the spread of error. The right to free expression can be stifled by such attitudes as surely as by legislation. Toleration does not mean silence. It requires a respectful attitude to those one believes to be wrong, not because they are entitled to be wrong, but because the Church in the name of Christ requires us to respect others unconditionally. Freedom of expression is a right to be used, and the more it is used properly to combat error and injustice, the less strange it will seem. Standing up to error is part of the responsible use of free expression.[47]

While the popes have concentrated on the moral dimension of freedom of expression, their teachings have not always been understood in liberal democracies. Given the exercise of political power by the Church in previous centuries, this is understandable. Some liberals regard a qualification on the use of a right as a qualification of the right itself. They are suspicious of any suggestion that rights may be abridged for religious reasons. They are more anxious about the dangers of religion to political liberty, about people being shut up and pushed around by the Church, than about the responsible use of liberties such as free expression. One consequence of this concern is that morality is divorced from politics in the name of liberty. Ironically, as I suggested above, this anxiety can induce the very silence that liberals fear from religious teachings.

Since Leo XIII wrote *Libertas* and *Rerum Novarum*, many of the issues he was addressing have been resolved. The separation of Church and State is now a fact; liberalism has established itself in Australia as the commonsense political position, as it has in most of the West; communism is barely a survival and socialism is not flourishing. In other words, the world and its threats both to democracy and to Catholic social teaching have changed considerably, but have not disappeared. The common good is under considerable strain in liberal political communities. Indeed, its very existence is denied in the context of social and political pluralism (whose version of the common good is to prevail?). It is no longer possible for the Church to exert authority as it previously could in matters such as censorship, and it is time that fears for democracy were directed elsewhere.

The right of free expression protects the voices of all in a secular democracy. Affirming this is important if the Church wants a Christian message is to be heard in liberal democracies. It has substantially made its peace with secularism around a host of welfare issues, such as justice for the poor. The political character of its position on issues of this kind seems to worry liberal secularists less than the Church's traditional views that morality is not all relative and that freedom brings responsibilities. Even the Church's warnings that we should not abuse free expression by lying, slander, offences against decency, and encouragement to civil disorder can still stir misgiving in a liberal. The big question about freedom of expression, however, should be addressed not to secularists but to Christians: will they choose to act responsibly and exercise that right to shape social change or merely be shaped by it?

Chapter 7

THE RIGHT TO CHOOSE AND FREELY MAINTAIN A STATE OF LIFE, MARRIED OR SINGLE, LAY OR RELIGIOUS

Marita Winters

Catholic Social Teaching holds that every person can freely choose and maintain a state of life, religious or lay, married or single. The Catholic tradition, and all the Church's social doctrine, is based on the view of the human person as of unique value, for "man ... is the only creature on earth which God willed for himself"[48].

The principles underpinning this right to choose and live a vocation are based in Christian anthropology, the foundations of which can be found in the Book of Genesis, detailing how each human person is created in the image and likeness of God. These principles can be understood by people regardless of their belief in God, and are enshrined in the Universal Declaration of Human Rights (UDHR) 1948.

The principle of human dignity is the most fundamental principle of Catholic social teaching. Human persons have been given a dignity beyond all other creatures. Because of their creation in God's image, man and woman share this dignity equally. Article 1 of the UDHR reflects the primacy of this right when it states that "All human beings are born free and equal in dignity and rights ..."

The principle of human equality states that social and cultural discrimination in fundamental rights is not compatible with God's design. Man and woman share the same faculties of reason and free will, and are entitled to receive equal fundamental rights.

Every person has an equal inherent dignity regardless of their sex, race, age, nationality, culture, employment or economic status, intelligence, health, achievements, origin or any other differentiating characteristics. The UDHR encapsulates this right in Article 2, and further rules out discrimination on the basis of the political, jurisdictional and international status of the person's country of origin.

The Catholic tradition proclaims that the human person is not only sacred but social. The centrepiece of society is the family, and it is here that the principle of association is seen at its most basic. A man and woman together as a couple are "the first form of communion between persons". [49] The *Catechism of the Catholic Church* declares of marriage: "By its very nature it is ordered to the good of the couple, as well as to the generation and education of children."[50]

The importance and centrality of the family with regard to the person and society is consistently articulated in the Scriptures. The UDHR reflects this tradition and asserts that:

> (1) Men and women of full age, without any limitation due to race, nationality or religion, have the right to marry and to found a family. They are entitled to equal rights as to marriage, during marriage and at its dissolution.
> (2) Marriage shall be entered into only with the free and full consent of the intending spouses.
> (3) The family is the natural and fundamental group unit of society and is entitled to protection by society and the State.[51]

The principle of the common good is the provision of social conditions which allow each individual to be nurtured and to flourish. The family is the basic building block of humanity and it is within the family that children "develop their potentialities, become aware of their dignity, and prepare to face their unique and individual destiny"[52].

The principle of participation, whereby a person exercises his right and duty to contribute to society, begins with the family and extends to all other institutions for the human person is involved "in a complex network of relationships within modern societies".[53]

The choice of how a person lives his or her life, whether lay or religious, married or single, is a central one. It is also linked with a person's relationship with God. Each person must be free to make his or her choice, without any undue interference from the State or from other interested parties, including parents or relatives.

Catholic thinking, particularly since the Middle Ages, has placed strong emphasis on consent freely given in choosing these basic life plans. It has stood against the treatment of women, serfs or other powerless parties as chattels to be married off for dynastic reasons or put away in convents when convenient, or used as breeding stock for the benefit of the powerful.

Thus medieval canon law was very strict on declaring invalid marriages where "consent" was coerced, whether for men and women.[54] The *Catechism of the Catholic Church* reflects this; that a married couple forms "the intimate partnership of life and love established by the Creator and governed by his laws; it is rooted in the conjugal covenant, that is, in their irrevocable personal consent."[55]

It was not just marriage that concerned the Church. In its long struggle for its rights with the State, the Church was also concerned to preserve independence for religious, for example by preventing monks being taken out of monasteries to be sent to the front line.

The Church has sought to encourage the role of religious, and believes their independence should not be obstructed by the State. A number of religious orders came to Australia around 1900, such as the De La Salle brothers and Ursuline sisters, expelled by anti-religious governments in Europe, governments which did not admit a right to religious life.

The religious vocation is presented in its diversity throughout Australia in the 41 orders of religious brothers, five institutes of religious brothers, 85 institutes of religious women, as well as seven institutes of consecrated life, eight Societies of Apostolic Life, and five newer Associations of Christ's Faithful in the Catholic Church.[56]

Religious priests, brothers and sisters choose to live their life for and with God and therefore have a special role in bearing witness to the faith. Pope John Paul II spoke of this when he addressed the religious of Australia during his visit in 1986:

> Brothers and sisters, religious of Australia, your Christian dignity depends principally not on what you do in service to the Church and to the world, but on what you are: consecrated followers of Christ, witnesses to a new and eternal life gained by the Redemption of Christ, imitators of the state of life which the Son of God took on in coming into this world. Because of your special relationship to Christ, you belong inseparably to the life and holiness of his Body, the Church.[57]

In general, Australians are relatively free to choose and maintain their state of life. With a person's right to choose his or her own vocation comes the right to choose when this decision is made, and in Australia, people are making their life choices later and later. For those who choose marriage and family life, the legal framework still exists to support marriage between a man and a woman as the norm, but since the middle of the last century significant changes have occurred. The federal parliament enacted legislation for marriages for the first time in 1959 with the *Matrimonial Causes Act*. In 1961 the *Marriage Act* provided for the formalities required for a lawful marriage, including marriageable age, marriage of minors, solemnisation of marriage, and foreign marriages.

The dissolution of marriage was brought into law with the 1975 reform of the *Family Law Act*. One of the most significant changes with this Act was the introduction of "no fault divorce". This Act also covered children born out of wedlock.

"Common law marriage" or "de facto marriage", referring to a relationship between two people who are not married but have been effectively living as husband and wife for a period of time, are not recognised in the *Marriage Act*. However, the Australian states and territories have enacted legislation covering issues such as property distribution, taxation, social welfare, pensions, and partner maintenance if such a relationship ends.

According to the Australian Bureau of Statistics, "Since the late 1970s there has been an increasing delay in the ages at which young people reach a range of milestones in the life cycle."[58] People are remaining single for longer, with young people not marrying until later than previous generations.[59] Others are finding themselves single again after a marriage or relationship breakdown.

The culture of marriage is declining, such that the traditional family is under attack with new forms of "marriage" and "family" being developed. Children are growing up in a wide variety of family types. Seven out of 10 children lived in intact families with their natural parents in 2003. About two in 10 children live in a lone-parent family and around one in 10 in step or blended families.[60]

The traditional understanding of marriage is in danger of being legislated away, with most Australian states giving formal recognition to "same-sex couples", with some even formally allowing them to adopt children (the biological children of one partner)[61].

Religious life is in decline, and pressure is sometimes exerted on individuals considering this way of life to reconsider his or her life choice. This influence is coming from family members and friends and the wider community as they see religious life as lonely or irrelevant, and religious communities aging and even dying out.

Yet the contribution of religious is just as important as ever. Pope John Paul II commented on this during his first visit to Australia:

> [H]ealth care, social welfare and the education of the young, which have been traditional apostolates of the religious of Australia, have become recognized as areas of responsibility for your Governments and now play a large part in their policies ... Your contribution in these fields has in fact become more important than

ever in the light of the rapid secularization taking place in Australian society as in other parts of the world. Within these fields, you are in a special way witnesses to the Gospel message of salvation in Christ Jesus[62].

All people can make a concrete commitment to solidarity and charity. Married couples and families need to be affirmed, and through the mutual support of husband and wife care can be given to both the older and younger generations. All people can promote and support policies with the family at the centre.

Young people can be encouraged to give due consideration to both lay and religious states of life, and family members can show their support for the person's free choice.

The Church and State must cooperate to ensure that the traditional definition of marriage as the union between one man and one woman remains. It is only through the love and fidelity of a husband and wife, with their family, that society will grow and flourish.

Chapter 8

THE RIGHT TO EDUCATION

Anthony Cleary

The right to education is a fundamental human right enshrined within and central to the United Nations Universal Declaration of Human Rights (UDHR, 1948). Inexhaustible in its potential value to both the individual and society, the right to education is essential to the informed exercise of all other social, civic, political and economic rights, for education can be a process of empowerment and self-actualisation.

The roots of all human rights, which are considered to be "universal, inviolable and inalienable"[63], are "to be found in the dignity that belongs to each human being."[64] By virtue of this inherent dignity, every individual has the right to an education that will afford them the principles of participation and the common good, ultimately leading them to fullness of life.

Fr William Byron SJ (1998) describes human dignity as the "bedrock principle"[65] or principle *par excellence* of Catholic social teaching, for it is from this that all other principles and rights proceed. This means that we not only acknowledge every person's inalienable right to education on the basis of what they might become but also because of who they are. The right to education does not spring solely from the fact that education can help students to realise their full potential, develop social consciences and become people who can contribute to their communities, but it also proceeds from their already existing dignity, a dignity arising from "Imago Dei".

We also educate, as was proposed by Socrates, in response to this existing human dignity which we hope to draw out, manifest to others, and perfect so that all might live life to the full. This notion is embedded within the etymological roots of education, which comes from the Latin *e-ducere* meaning "to lead or draw out."

According to the Second Vatican Council's declaration on Christian education, *Gravissimum Educationis* (1965) "a true education aims at the formation of the human person in the pursuit of his ultimate end and of the good of the societies of which, as man, he is a member."[66] This affirms the long-held view that education should be directed towards both individual and social ends. In Western nations this translates to the fundamental goal of equipping individuals with virtues and good habits to function optimally as members of just, tolerant and free societies and to work towards this end.

Education has long been regarded as the acquisition of knowledge. While acquiring knowledge is a significant part of education, promoting a love of learning, developing individual talents and social skills, and nurturing a person's critical capacity to distinguish information and make decisions on the basis of sound reasoning are all important underlying aspects of education.

Through education students learn more than reading, writing and arithmetic. They can learn how to responsibly exercise personal freedom for the betterment of self and others, how to function in and contribute to society, develop their capacity for critical thinking and moral reasoning, and experience the "full development of the human personality."[67]

Education must address a diversity of needs and nurture the material, moral and spiritual capacities of the individual. If a person acquires knowledge but not the capacity for moral reasoning, he or she is diminished personally. Harm can be done to others; a point affirmed in Theodore Roosevelt's reputed assertion that to educate a person in mind and not in morals is to educate a menace to society. Both knowledge and moral reasoning are indispensable for the development of self and for one to be of true service to others and society.

True education is transformative, a source of personal and social change, as it stimulates learning and cognitive development as well as nurturing emotional and moral intelligence. Schools, colleges and universities cannot just be places of instruction and cognitive learning. Rather they must be communities in which all facets of the human personality are drawn out. They must preserve and develop human values and abilities that build the kind of future we want for our children and society.

Given that we live in a shrinking global village of multiple communities and cultures, our young people must not only learn about their rights and responsibilities as Australian citizens but must be equipped with the skills, attitudes and values needed to enable them to become responsible global citizens. In order for this to be achieved, education systems must give a higher priority to articulating universal truths and principles instead of cultural relativism and to promoting mutual respect, understanding and cooperation, reiterating that "every person – regardless of race, sex, age national origin, religion ... is worthy of respect."[68]

It is through education that people are afforded the opportunity of participation, for all individuals not only have a right but a "duty to participate in society, seeking together the common good and well being of all, especially the poor and vulnerable."[69] This principle, fully expressed, requires the individual to know what the common good is, to desire it, to respect it, not only in relation to his or her own rights but to the rights of others, and to have the means and the skills necessary to pursue that good. According to William Byron, "the common good is always oriented towards the progress of persons ... founded on truth, built up in justice and animated by love."[70] Ultimately, the common good "corresponds to the highest of human instincts" yet it is difficult to attain, requiring constant attention and effort, for many are driven by vested self-interest rather than seeking "the good of others as though it were one's own."[71]

A commitment to the common good must be the focus of and inform educational programs, practices and priorities rather than those which are driven by relativism or based on a given economic ideology or imposed by any powerful political, religious or cultural group.

While governments have generally agreed about their responsibilities in relation to the right to education, this commitment has often been threatened by the push to apply market principles to education, leaving some deprived of meaningful educational opportunities. There is a disparity in the education available to people on the basis of their socio-economic status and this is evidenced in participation rates and achievement levels. This is especially true for people living in remote rural and indigenous communities. It is apparent therefore that achieving the basic right to education for all remains one of the greatest moral challenges of our times.

Education can reduce intellectual isolation and contribute to the creation of a more just and equitable society, one underpinned by the principle of preferential protection for the poor and vulnerable, not however when it is driven by economic rationalism. It is imperative that governments and education systems renew their commitment to the mandate and spirit of the UDHR (Articles 26.1-26.3) so as to ensure not only that everyone has access to education but that it is of adequate quality.

A lack of education represents more than a diminishment of future choices or a stifling of talent; it is a violation of the first and deepest principle of human rights, the principle of human dignity. Where the lack of education is imposed upon the child from outside, as is the case in societies in which girls and women are denied education, it is oppression. Denial of education for whatever reason is a form of oppression. Where the lack of education emerges from the student's own attitude, laziness or a chronic contempt for schooling, it is a form of self-injury as serious as physical self-harm. James Franklin argues that "staying deliberately ignorant by refusing to learn anything at school harms the intellectual part of the personality, and it's wrong whether you consent or not ... deliberate ignorance is a perversion of our nature, a failure to develop what is good."[72]

Of concern is the view held by some educators and sociologists that the nature of schooling and education is inherently repressive, alienating students from self-learning and self-discovery, creating a culture of meaninglessness. Such views arise when schools are perceived as vehicles of capitalism, competition or increasingly in some parts of the world, indoctrination.

Education should never be a vehicle of indoctrination, whether that indoctrination is the intent of religious extremists or political ideologists. Such an education runs counter to the purpose of education for it does not respect individual freedom nor does it nurture critical thinking. While the custodians of such schools (including some modern madrassahs) hold the view that they are educating for a better world, we must question their notion of a better world. It is true that there are diverse views and visions about what makes a better world, however there are ample warnings about the dangers of attempting to impose a new world order. The utopia is soon a dystopia, the vision a delusion, the dream a nightmare. We need to be mindful of and sensitive to the damage that can be done by an education which does not seek to influence both the intellect and the will while recognising and respecting the essential nature of both human dignity, freedom of the individual and the common good.

Rather than being vehicles of indoctrination schools can and should be centres of justice, freedom and empowerment, providing a supportive and nurturing environment, which "contributes to the development of students' sense of self-worth, enthusiasm for learning and optimism for the future."[73] Education has a great capacity to change and sustain the direction of humankind, therefore places of learning must be dedicated to the common good of humanity, where critical thinking, moral reasoning, service, citizenship and empowerment become the norms.

The 1982 document of the Sacred Congregation for Catholic Education, *Lay Catholics in Schools*, reminds us that "every person has a right to an integral education, an education which responds to all of the needs of the human person."[74] Education must serve to develop and nurture individual personalities, affirming their universal rights and acknowledging those of others, to fully, actively and meaningfully participate in and contribute to our modern and increasingly complex and diverse society. By virtue of our human dignity all people have an inalienable right to an education which will draw out their inherent talents and capacities, so that they might have life and have it to the full.

Chapter 9

THE RIGHT TO PETITION GOVERNMENT FOR THE REDRESS OF GRIEVANCES

Paul Russell

The broad grouping of natural rights covered by this category could most accurately be described as rights of participation. We have the right to participate in the processes of governance because every decision made by our representatives affects us in some way. The inalienable dignity of every person demands of itself the right of every person to enjoy freedom, justice and peace. So, whenever an injustice of some form creates an affront to dignity, there needs to be some formal avenue of redress. In fact, we could say that a right is not a right at all unless it is accompanied by the ability to seek corrective justice.

At first glance we might consider "petition" and "redress of grievances" to indicate that these rights exist only in an "after-the-fact" manner. Some action, some law, some situation is found to be unjust, and individuals or groups act to seek change. While only part of the picture, this is nonetheless an indispensable element critical to the functions of accountability at all levels of government and organised society.

Petition and redress can be viewed as two sides of the same coin. We can formally petition our legislative representatives and, if unsuccessful, vote them out at the next election. We can access complaint procedures if poorly treated by government departments and, if unsuccessful, we can appeal to an ombudsman. We can take an issue to a court and, if unsuccessful, appeal to a higher level.

The UN International Covenant on Civil and Political Rights (ICCPR, Art. 2 (3)) charges the State with the task of ensuring both the rights and freedoms of the individual and "effective remedy" should they be violated. While some levels of government are either fully or partially accountable to a higher government none can entirely dispense with their responsibility to guarantee these rights.

The hundred years and more prior to the proclamation of *Rerum Novarum* by Pope Leo XIII in 1891 had seen rapid changes to industrial and economic organisation which brought significant upheaval to the divisions of labour and capital and, consequently, to family life and society. *Rerum Novarum* itself could be seen as a petition, writ large, to governments of all persuasions for a systematised protection of labour, the home, the family and the rights to freedom that would only be recognised in international covenants many years later. Though only formally acknowledged 100 years later by Pope John Paul II in *Centesimus Annus*, democratic government was implicitly recognised as the only form of government that can effectively guarantee these rights and protect its citizens.

The right to petition government for the redress of grievances provides some of the basic inbuilt protections that guarantee not only the rights of the individual, but also the proper functioning of democratic principles. The very fact that we can act to protect our rights and seek to have grievances resolved is a corrective to the improper use of power and the lack of justice in policy. One of the early signs that a government is failing its obligations to its citizens occurs when these rights to participation are denied or limited without due cause.

The line, "Yonder sits the Fourth Estate, and they are more important than them all," is attributed to the great Irish political theorist, Edmund Burke, referring to the press gallery of the British House of Commons. Clearly Burke understood that the press has a significant role to play in the protection of rights and freedoms. The right to freedom of the press is probably our greatest guarantee of the right to participation in the process of government. It offers us not only a vital window into the actions of government but also a variety of critical opinion on the effectiveness of policy and a potent vehicle for redress of grievances.

This technological age increases the accountability of government bringing with it a globalised view on world events. One need only think of the Tiananmen Square pro-democracy protests in China in 1989, to see the effect that the international press exerts on governments. The image of the lone protestor standing peacefully in front of four advancing tanks in June that year remains a potent symbol of the ongoing struggles in the most populous nation on earth. Reports of the death toll of the April demonstrations vary from a few hundred to tens of thousands. The protestors' concerns were highlighted most poignantly in the days following the massacre when the Communist government banned the international press from Beijing and the Chinese mainland and severely censored reporting in government-controlled media.

One of the first signs that a government is reneging on its duty to be open, accountable and democratic, is most often seen in unjust restrictions being placed on the media; either restrictions on what can be published or restrictions on access to information, or both. (Another example from China is the State blocking internet access to foreign sites critical of the current regime.)

We cannot question the fact that governments do need to retain the right to quarantine some information from public view; however, this should be kept to a minimum. The codification of Freedom of Information legislation in all Australian States in recent decades is a welcome acknowledgement of such rights. The access (or lack of access) to information via freedom of information requests is now, in many respects, a barometer of good government.

Article 21 of the ICCPR guarantees the right to peaceful assembly. Public demonstration is both an opportunity to raise public awareness on an issue and to demonstrate to government that the grievance concerned has wide public interest. The international covenant argues that no restriction should be placed on the exercise of this right except that they conform to the laws of the land and do not pose a threat to public order, health or morals or the rights and freedoms of others. A number of Australian States have legislated to protect the right to peaceful assembly, codifying therein the responsibilities of organisers in respect to public order.

The ICCPR does, however, prescribe certain particular (and hopefully rare) occasions when a State may suspend the exercise of such rights to participation described above. Article 4 cites times of "public emergency" which threaten the life of the nation when, and only when, the existence of such a situation is officially proclaimed. In such cases the higher obligation of the State to protect itself (and, thereby, its citizens) may require the temporary suspension (or dilution) of other rights. One need only think of censorship of the press in times of war as a potent example. The prerequisite proclamation of such an emergency protects citizens from the inappropriate use of power which must be restored as soon as possible after the emergency has passed.

Another development in our times that supports the right of petition and access to redress for grievances can be found in the improvement of government departmental codes of conduct and procedures for dealing with complaints from the public. Complaint procedures in most, if not all, government departments are made available to clients and are widely promoted. The fact that every client has a right to complain and has a recognised avenue to do so creates an atmosphere of transparency and accountability, as does the access to independent review via growing numbers of independent ombudsman.

Further evidence of governments providing positive measures to protect our rights can be found in our judiciary and in civil law. The provision of penalties in the criminal code and compensation for injustice in civil matters creates both a disincentive to unjust behaviour and a positive redress for victims. The independence of the judiciary from political influence and the existence of higher courts of appeal reflect Pope John Paul II's thoughts when he points out that, "it is preferable that each power be balanced by other powers and by other spheres of responsibility which keep it within proper bounds". (*Centesimus Annus* n44)

The right to petition government for the redress of grievances, like many genuine rights, remains latent for the majority of citizens most of the time: we are glad they exist in times of need, but they rarely feature in our day-to-day existence. That is not to say, however, that, like a good book, they simply "gather dust" between use. Such rights remain a constant bulwark against the possibility of abuses of power while at the same time acting to protect individuals and society as a whole, guaranteeing our freedom, justice and peace.

Chapter 10

THE RIGHT TO A NATIONALITY

Andrew Hamilton

The most significant feature of Papal social teaching about the right to a nationality is that it has little to say on the subject. Episcopal statements and documents of Roman dicasteries, with which I shall not deal here, do contribute a little more. But Papal and Conciliar documents do offer illuminating insights on the basis of which something useful might be said.

The relative silence reflects the nature of Catholic social teaching which responds to questions that Catholics ask when their society changes. The way in which the teaching develops will be influenced both by what they see and by the questions that they ask about what they see.

Questions that might lead us to insist that people have the right to a nationality have been asked only relatively recently. They are posed when we notice the faces of stateless persons, of persons discriminated against as a result of the formation of new states, and of refugees driven away when they seek asylum. It is only relatively recently that such predicaments have attracted public attention and Catholic reflection. In its origins Catholic social teaching focused on other questions, particularly the effects that industrialisation had on human welfare and relationships in the developed world.

In its early stages, too, Catholic social teaching had little to say about nations and about their relationship to their citizens. This is understandable because it is not the Church's business to develop a systematic political philosophy. In its origins the teaching was Eurocentric. It took for granted the stable existence of European nations and of their overseas colonies, associating nationality with the coincidence of historical circumstances and of a shared language and cultural history. From this perspective it is difficult to see how stateless people or refugees could be entitled to nationality in a land whose language and history was alien to them. So although Councils, Synods and Popes have noted the predicament of and claims made by migrant workers, refugees and minority groups, they have not considered that displaced people should be given nationality in the places to which they come.

But if we reflect on the right to a nationality, we shall find in Catholic social teaching many illuminating insights. They all flow from the central convictions that each human being is infinitely precious and that each human being is social. In this view, human beings are not simply individuals who are defined in isolation from other people. The unique and irreplaceable dignity of each human being, here grounded in God's creative and redemptive love, is realised in our relationships to God, to one another and to the world. This belief implies that we thrive as human beings only when we are supported by others and cooperate with them. We also need to belong to groups – families, clubs, workplaces, shires, unions and nations. Through them we can find the necessities of life, such as security, food and shelter, the capacity to develop our gifts and take responsibility for our lives, and to develop our relationships with one another and with God. Ultimately, we are bound to the whole of humanity.

The unique personal value of each human being and the need to cooperate to realise our humanity has implications for national identity. Nations are important social groups because they shape the conditions under which human beings may flourish. They provide security and give structure to public relationships between citizens. But they exist for the development of each human being, beginning with the weakest. Because human beings are responsible to one another, nations too are responsible to each other to ensure that the most impoverished and unprotected can live in a way consistent with their human dignity. Faces have precedence over flags.

Thus the relationship of nations to the person, like the relationship of any subordinate group, is to promote the good of persons, especially the most unprotected. But because persons are social, the good of each person needs to take into account the good of the whole body, which is again composed of persons. So the responsibility of nations is first to its citizens, but cannot be confined to them, because their good is reached fully only in a just and equitable world. This means that unprotected citizens anywhere can make a claim on the national state.

This general framework of thought was developed further in the Encyclicals of John XXIII, Paul VI and John Paul II. They reflected on a world where issues of peace and of development became central. In particular, two concepts useful for discussing nationality were developed: solidarity and participation. Solidarity implies that nations are responsible for people outside their own boundaries. Participation establishes what people may claim from governments.

The concept of solidarity was first drawn on by Paul VI, and was substantially developed by John Paul II. By then it had an aura derived from the Solidarity Movement in Poland. The two Popes built on concepts of friendship, of social charity, and of a culture of love developed in earlier Encyclicals. Solidarity supposes that we feel an initial sympathy with others who suffer injustice or deprivation. This feeling of sympathy with those unjustly treated leads us to a properly moral response. We recognise that we are bound to our neighbours because we share a common humanity, and we commit ourselves to act in ways that redress the injustice they suffer. The initial movement of our hearts leads to a practical commitment to make the world more just.

Solidarity between nations implies that they will share their resources in order to ensure that people who are deprived or oppressed can live in accordance with their human dignity. When appealing to national governments to act out of solidarity, the Encyclicals sometimes describe this responsibility as one of charity, sometimes as one of justice. They urge the receiving nations, for example, to sign a charter protecting the rights of migrant workers. This implies that justice demands acting in a way that safeguards human dignity. Elsewhere they appeal to nations to exercise charity towards migrant workers and refugees. Both forms of response are grounded in international solidarity. The initial affective response naturally leads to charitable action. Because solidarity also includes moral commitment, nations are morally responsible to cooperate for the welfare of human beings beyond their own borders, particularly the most disadvantaged.

If solidarity means that states have responsibility both for their own citizens and for those who make a legitimate claim on them, the concept of participation grounds the right that persons can make on nations, even on nations to which they do not belong. The concept of participation expresses people's need, and so right, to live actively in society and culture in a way that protects their own religion, political beliefs, language and cultural practices. It also expresses their right to take responsibility for shaping their own life and that of their families. The responsibility of the national state to ensure that the members of different groups – workers, employers, minority groups – are able to live and work equitably in society is also treated through the concept of participation.

Papal Encyclicals do occasionally refer to the responsibility of states to allow groups like refugees and minority groups to participate in society without discrimination. Although they do not claim explicitly that people unjustly deprived of the ability to participate in their own nation have the right to a nationality elsewhere, it is hard to avoid that conclusion. How else can people participate fully in a society if it is not possible for them to claim nationality? Without it their status is precarious, and they are easily treated as second-class citizens. We can say, then, that in the modern world one of the conditions of life with full human dignity, in which rights are grounded, is the enjoyment of nationality.

Nationality is a right that often cannot be vindicated. In Catholic teaching the world community has a responsibility for those who cannot live with full human dignity. This responsibility is accepted by those who sign various international treaties and conventions. Perhaps the United Nations Convention on the Status of Refugees is most helpful for reflection on the right to a nationality. It requires its signatories in defined circumstances to offer effective protection to those who cannot avail themselves of the protection of their own governments. Protection includes the guarantee of a full life, including shelter, security, and the capacity to get on with one's life. This will normally be for the short term, but if it is impossible for people to return to their own nations protection may imply the acquisition of another nationality. They will ordinarily receive nationality from the nation on which they make a justified claim for protection. If nationality is defined by blood or race, and those given protection cannot receive nationality, they will feel discriminated against and will never feel invited to participate fully in society. This has long been evident in the lives of fourth-generation residents in a nation, who must carry special papers and take names that will identify them as of alien descent. They always feel outsiders, are always vulnerable as scapegoats in hard times.

On the basis of Papal social teaching, then, we might argue that all human persons have the right to a nationality, and that the international community has the responsibility to enable them to enjoy this right if they are indefinitely prevented from enjoying it in their nation of birth. The challenge remains to vindicate this right, particularly in situations where there are large numbers of stateless people and where there is no effective will to address their situation.

Note on sources.

The early Papal Encyclicals establish the bases of Catholic Social teaching while discussing economic relationships in industrialising societies. Only after the Second World War in a world characterised by fear of nuclear war and by problems of development, do relationships between nations receive extended attention in John XXIII's encyclicals, *Pacem in Terris* and *Mater et Magistra*. The crucial spur to further development is the Vatican II document, *Gaudium et Spes* which develops the understanding of human dignity and treats of international relationships. Its ideas are developed further in the Encyclicals of Paul VI and of John Paul II, most notably in *Octagesimo Adveniens* and *Sollicitudo Rei Sociali*, which begin to integrate the framework of human rights with the framework of human dignity. They explore the implications of notions of solidarity and of participation, applying them to persons and to nations.

Chapter 11

THE RIGHT TO HAVE ACCESS TO THE MEANS OF A LIVELIHOOD, BY MIGRATION WHEN NECESSARY

Brenda Hubber

It is written in the Bible, "God created man and woman in his image";[75] and it is from this basic tenet the principles of Catholic social teaching are derived.

Being *created by God*, all humans have the right to life. However, this right is short lived if people do not have access to all the things needed to sustain that life; that is, water, food, clothing and shelter.

As children, we are generally provided for by our parents and families. As independent adults, we are entitled to a livelihood that will afford us all the necessities of life.

Being *made in God's image*, we are made equal in the sight of God. As equals, we are entitled to equal access to the world's resources, including the means of production and a livelihood. But, having access to the means of production does not imply ownership of the capital or means of production but, in most cases, access through the supply of labour. For those unable to compete in the employment market, such as the disabled or the aged, they are still entitled to an income that affords them a reasonable standard of living.

It may seem utopian to suggest all are entitled to equal access to the resources of the world but that does not mean it should not be aspired to, as far as is consistent with normal rights to free action. How we treat the most marginalised in our society is as important as the struggle for greater equality; and is our responsibility under the Common Good.

The right to a livelihood is enshrined in Article 23 of the Universal Declaration of Human Rights along with the rights to choice of employment; equitable wages; reasonable work conditions; collective bargaining; and protection against unemployment.

However, some 57 years earlier than the Universal Declaration, Pope Leo XIII in his encyclical *Rerum Novarum* (Of New Things) explored the relationship between workers and the means of production. He strongly defended the rights of individuals to own land (i.e. the means of production); and questioned why the relationship between the wealthy and the workers had to be so oppositional.

At the time this encyclical was issued, the Vatican had just been relieved of large tracts of land by the Italian government. Freed from the temporal duties of running a large state, Pope Leo XIII was more able to reflect on the social condition of the working class and to take a more principled stance on their treatment.[76] For too long, workers (including women and children) had been working long hours, in dangerous work situations, for wages that were hardly putting bread on their tables.

As workers, we are entitled to a just wage for the work we perform. The minimum wage should be "sufficient to enable the worker … to have the benefits of survival, good health, security and modest comfort. Wages must also allow workers to provide for the future and acquire the property needed for the support of a family."[77]

In Australia, the federal minimum wage is currently calculated at approximately $22,500 for a single worker and up to $42,600 for a family of four with dual incomes. Where wages do not meet minimum standards, they are supplemented with appropriate government transfers in the form of family tax rebates and family allowance payments. These supplements should not be viewed as charity but as *members of our society receiving their due*; that is, parents receiving sufficient remuneration for raising children on behalf of society.

The family has long been recognised as the central building block of society[78]. It is through the family that we, as individuals, become active members of society. The way our parents bring us up, the education they can afford to give us, and the work ethic they instil in us, shape us as future workers. Thus, access to a livelihood that supports the family is important for the healthy development of individuals, families, communities and the wider society.

The stability of the family is paramount for the stability of society so families should be protected against conditions that destabilise it. Long work hours, poor wages and job insecurity can be sources of family tension and detract from people's enjoyment of life, their standard of living and their ability to reach their full potential. Thus, the dignity of workers should be protected through reasonable work conditions and leave entitlements.

All people have the right to participate in society and this includes the right not to be excluded from paid employment. If people are excluded from paid employment then they are denied access to a decent livelihood and productive activity that could lead to professional and personal fulfilment.

Protection against unemployment can come in the form of greater job security; or, if unemployed, social security payments. However, social security should not be considered a reasonable livelihood, as it is approximately half the minimum wage. The long-term effects of exclusion and welfare reliance can be seen in the poor living conditions and inter-generational disadvantage experienced by indigenous Australians today.

With all rights, come responsibilities. As people of God, we are expected to use our skills and talents not only for the betterment of ourselves and our families but also for the betterment of the communities and societies in which we live (for the Common Good).

Almsgiving is another way of contributing to the Common Good. With almsgiving, we are not asked to give of anything we do not need ourselves; but when our own necessities are met "it becomes a duty to give to the indigent out of what remains".[79] Though not required by law to give to charity, we are encouraged through tax deductions.

On the right to migrate, if necessary, to gain access to the means of a livelihood – the Universal Declaration of Human Rights includes the right to a nationality; the right not to be denied a nationality; the right to travel outside your home country and the right to change nationality, if so desired (Articles 13 & 15) – but it does not articulate the right to migrate so as to gain access to a livelihood.

It is not even specifically spelt out in *Rerum Novarum*. In arguing the rightness of landownership, Pope Leo XIII observed that people "work harder and more readily when they work on that which belongs to them"[80]. Consequently, this makes people more attached to their homeland. People "would cling to the country in which they were born, for no one would exchange [their] country for a foreign land if [their] own afforded [them] the means of living a decent and happy life"[81].

However, if their homeland did not afford them "the means of living a decent and happy life", then they would be quite within their rights to migrate. Thus, the right to migrate to gain access to the means of a livelihood is not an absolute right like "the right to life, liberty and security of person"[82]. It is only invoked in the event a person is denied access to a livelihood in their home country.

This is a moot point because most people would have access to some form of livelihood. The questions are whether that livelihood respects their human dignity, allows them to reach their full potential and provides them with an acceptable standard of living for themselves and, if applicable, for their families also.

Most Australians who migrate overseas to work do so, not because they have to but because they can choose to, for better employment opportunities. The same would also generally apply to migrant workers coming to Australia.

Migration is a natural phenomenon. God decreed, "Be fruitful and multiply, and fill the earth." By migrating, all species move from overused areas, ensuring their survival. However, migration is often cast in negative terms – migrants will steal our jobs; they will bring poverty and crime. Innumerable reports have proved the contrary. Migrants are generally hard working and motivated to succeed. The Australian Immigration website quotes the billions of dollars that migration brings to the federal budget each year.[83]

With increased globalisation, it has been suggested that migration has increased. It is true that the number of migrants has doubled since 1970; but despite some of the most turbulent times in the twentieth century, migration has remained around 3 per cent of the total world population at any given time.[84]

It is also true skilled business migration to Australia has trebled over the last ten years. This has raised considerable concern about the exploitation of migrant workers and its effect of reducing the wages of local workers. With current Workplace Relations legislation, this is highly likely to continue.

Australian workers, while defending local rights against erosion, need to also lobby for Australia to sign an international convention to protect not only the livelihood and human dignity of migrant workers and their families but also to maintain the integrity of local livelihoods and work conditions for future Australians.

Liberatore, the initial drafter of *Rerum Novarum*, recognised, all those years ago, the need for "an international agreement of some kind"[85] to protect the rights of all workers whether they migrated or not. There is now an International Convention on the Protection of the Rights of All Migrant Workers and Members of their Families; but it has the unenviable record of taking the longest time, out of the seven core UN conventions, to come into action. Adopted in December 1990, it was not ratified until July 2003.

Only 34 of the 125 states that have signed all six other conventions have signed the Migrant Workers Convention. Many nation states, like Australia, feel many rights are already articulated under other UN conventions; however, the Migrant Workers Convention contains many rights unique to the situations in which migrant workers and their families may find themselves.

It is a sad indictment on the human race that protection of migrant workers is not universal and a convention, like this, needs to exist. The Migrant Workers Convention needs to be ratified by more countries before workers of the world can expect any measure of equality in this ever evolving globalisation.

If managed properly, globalisation has the potential to lift millions out of poverty. The first stage has been the free flow of capital and goods. The next is the freer movement of labour, which will hopefully lead to all people having a more equitable share in the world's prosperity.[86]

It should be noted that the vast majority of the world's population does not migrate, yet we all benefit from this phenomenon. The evolution of the human race has only been possible through people being willing to migrate and countries being prepared to accept them.

As for the Catholic Church, it is important to remain independent of any specific political view to maintain moral authority. However, it should not stand by silently as new injustices evolve.

Chapter 12

THE RIGHT OF ASSOCIATION AND PEACEFUL ASSEMBLY

Michael Hogan

At first glance these two rights seem very closely related. Both refer to the freedom of people to come together with others for certain purposes (association), or in certain places (assembly). Both are central to the health of a liberal democratic society because they protect free political organisation, without which democracy is a fraud. Christian social teaching has been much more concerned over the past century with the right of association, seeming to regard the right of assembly as not under serious threat.

The right of association

As a freedom essential for democracy, the right of association is an encouragement for people to come together in the widest range of cultural meetings, sporting clubs, pressure groups, professional colleges, trade unions, and legitimate political parties. If one returns to the seminal document of *Rerum Novarum* (1891), to which the Catholic Truth Society gave the extra title of "The Workers' Charter", it is clear that the right of association is presented as the central mechanism that can improve the welfare of working people. The specific association for the Church at that time, although others are mentioned, is the trade union. The Church came down unequivocally against those States, and employers' organisations, that tried to make trade unions illegal in the nineteenth century (and well into the twentieth, for that matter).

Although the right of workers to form trade unions is vigorously defended in *Rerum Novarum*, Catholic social teaching at the time clearly regarded some forms of such association as healthy and others as harmful. Looking back to the medieval craft guilds for a precedent, the most desirable form of trade union was one formed by the association of workers within the framework of a network of Church associations. Trade unions permeated by socialist or Masonic ideology were particularly to be avoided, if not condemned. Preference for Catholic trade unions continued to be a feature of Catholic social teaching, although by the time Pope Pius XI issued the 40th anniversary social encyclical, *Quadragesimo Anno*, in 1931, it was clear that Catholic workers often had only the choice of a secular trade union: "It belongs to the Bishops to permit Catholic workingmen to join these unions, where they judge that circumstances render it necessary and there appears no danger for religion" (p. 13).

In Australia, the teaching of *Rerum Novarum* was received by the Catholic community with considerable enthusiasm in 1891. Catholics were already occupying leadership positions in many secular trade unions, so that in many ways the Australian Catholic Church was well ahead of the European experience that informed the encyclical. Despite considerable suspicion of socialist influences in the local labour movement, Cardinal Moran eventually came to encourage working men to participate in the parliamentary wing of the trade union movement – the new Labor Party (there was no challenge to their freedom to join the other main parties of the time as well). The Australian Church was always ambivalent about the European model of separatist Catholic political and industrial organisation, seeing it as exacerbating an already disturbing sectarian division in society. One of the benefits of this approach has been that leaders of the other main Christian denominations have normally not regarded this as a sectarian issue. They may not always have been as enthusiastic as Catholic leaders in defending the freedom of association, but there is little difference in their social teaching on the matter. The church, like democracy, thrives when people are encouraged to participate actively in their fields of interest.

During the 1930s and 1940s, when European ideas of (separatist) Catholic Action were again coming to prominence in the Australian Church, the official teaching of the Australian bishops suggested an industry-based set of associations that brought employers, employees and consumers into a united body to take the place of the conflict-model of employers versus unions. This ideal of "industrial councils" or "vocational groups" was offered in the early social justice statements[87] – the *Bishops Statement on Social Justice* (1940), *Justice Now!* (1941), *For Freedom* (1942) and *Pattern for Peace* (1943). By 1947, however, when a wave of post-war industrial conflict was paralysing the nation, the bishops' document on *Peace in Industry* strongly repeated the doctrine of *Rerum Novarum* defending the right of workers to form trade unions and to invoke the strike weapon under certain conditions. Equally strongly the document condemned the misuse of such associations by Communists.

By the final quarter of the twentieth century, Australian Catholic social teaching in the statements of the Catholic Commission for Justice and Peace (CCJP) was starting to move beyond a concentration on the right of association as a cure for the world's ills or the welfare of workers. In the Second Vatican Council of the 1960s, Chapter 4 of the pastoral constitution, *Gaudium et Spes*, had encouraged the participation of Catholics in all kinds of political associations, while recognising that in a pluralist society they would often be pulling in different directions. Following this lead, and without denying what had been said earlier about trade unions and other associations, the CCJP emphasised that a reliance on existing associations would not solve the problems of unemployment (1979), or poverty (1980), or peace (1985, 1986). The point was made explicitly in *Changing Australia* (1983): "Sometimes new organisations and new types of actions are needed". [88] We ought to contemplate associations with a worldwide concern, not just groups with narrow sectional or national interest that have dominated in the past. This has continued as the central theme of social teaching on the right of association for the body that succeeded the CCJP, the Bishops' Committee for Justice and Peace. Catholic bishops have resisted attempts by Commonwealth governments to restructure the industrial relations landscape by crippling the trade union movement. Yet, while freedom of association is strongly defended, the Church asserts that it is not sufficient by itself to bring about a truly just society.

The right of assembly

There is a paradox at the heart of any discussion of Christian social teaching on the right of assembly. Within the British tradition of civil rights that Australia inherited, it was the churches themselves whose interests led to the evolution of the present legal protection for the right of citizens to come together in public places. The rights of the established Church of England were seen as overriding the religious freedom of assembly for the Church of Scotland in the sixteenth and seventeenth centuries, as for Nonconformist or Dissenting worshippers in the seventeenth and eighteenth centuries, while it was not until well into the nineteenth century that Catholic Emancipation legislation conceded full rights of assembly to Catholics. Yet, now that the rights of assembly for worship have been effectively conceded, Christian social teaching virtually ignores the wider question of the rights of assembly for the sake of political protest.

At the same time, there is an argument that, even in a society as free as Australia, the right of assembly is the most circumscribed and restricted of all the fundamental human rights. The major churches are free to assemble in churches and to mark religious occasions with processions on public streets. Meanwhile, development applications for a new mosque or temple for minority religious groups are likely to face concerted community opposition and local government obstruction. As a government report into religious discrimination in New South Wales pointed out: "An unfamiliar religious group would be naïve to suppose that it will be able to establish itself within a local community without some opposition and at its first attempt".[89] Such religious groups very rarely find champions among leaders of the main Australian Christian churches.

Restrictions on the right of assembly are more obvious in the matter of political protests and demonstrations. It is stating the obvious that the rights of some people may need to be restricted in practice when they conflict with the equally clear rights of others. Governments thus have customarily placed legislative boundaries on the unfettered freedom of speech, the press or assembly – or rights to work, nationality, or social welfare. In the issue of freedom of assembly the normal constraint is that public spaces and streets may be used for political protest as long as such demonstrations do not interfere with the normal rights of pedestrian or vehicular traffic. While acknowledging the virtue of this principle, it is immediately clear that it is capable of effectively denying the freedom or right of assembly. It depends how it is administered, and what measure of community inconvenience should be tolerated. In Australia, at both Commonwealth and State/Territory level, there has been almost no attempt by governments to spell out general principles. Discretion is left to the police beforehand or the courts afterwards. As Gaze and Jones have pointed out, there is an absence of positive protection for this right, and "the liberty to assemble is very much a residual right".[90] When a planned political protest needs a police permit or prior notification that can result in effective denial, as is the case in most Australian jurisdictions, one could argue that the right of freedom of assembly does not exist at all. There is *permission*, not freedom, to protest.

Leaders of the major Australian churches have made almost no contribution to the debate about how the right of political assembly may legitimately be restricted. Almost the only Christian voices have been minority ones – from small religious denominations such as the Quakers, or from radicalised minority groups within the major churches, such as the defence of demonstrations against the Vietnam war and the conscription of Australians in Val Noone's *Disturbing the War* (1993). The Christian Church leaves itself open to the accusation that once its own freedom of assembly is guaranteed there is no further need for care.

Chapter 13

THE RIGHT TO WORK

Ian Blandthorn

The United Nations Universal Declaration of Human Rights states at Article 23 that "everyone has the right to work". The Church also asserts that all people have the right to work. This right is spelt out in the Bible and in Church documents.

The book of Genesis tells us that men and women are created in the image of God.[91] Genesis also says that men and women should be fruitful and multiply and fill the earth and subdue it[92]. While this statement does not refer explicitly to work it nevertheless clearly directs people to be active in the world and to work to better the world. In doing so men and women reflect the very action of the Creator of the world in whose image they are made.

Pope John Paul II said in *Laborem Exercens* that work is "a fundamental dimension of human existence on earth" and the means by which men and women implement the command in Genesis to subdue the earth.[93]

Genesis makes it clear that men and women have a pre-eminent place in the social order. Work honours the Creator's gifts and the talents received from him. It is the human response to the gifts of God.

As Pope Paul VI said, people have a right and a duty to develop themselves, and through work they can grow in humanity, enhance their personal worth and become more of a person and a spiritual being.[94]

At its most basic paid work provides the means by which people accumulate the resources to live and function in society. However, work provides for much more than that. It is the means by which a person develops their individual expression and creativity. It is the means by which a person realises their potential as a member of society. Work is a way of ensuring we have a continuing participation in God's creation.

Whilst different jobs generate different levels of status and remuneration in terms of community acknowledgement all work, provided it is carried out with the free will of the individual, confers status and dignity. This applies whether the job is well paid, lowly paid or even unpaid, whether it is manual or intellectual in its nature and whether it is full time or less than full time.

Work is our right and our vocation. Work is the way we express ourselves and grow as persons. It is necessary for the full flowering of the human person. Work gives man identity and dignity. In *Laborem Exercens* work is described as an obligation or duty which falls upon all people.[95]

Human work accords with God's will. People must work, not only because the Creator has demanded it but also because it enhances their own humanity and dignity. All people have a duty to use the talents afforded them by the Creator to the fullest extent.

The right to work is realised through purposeful activity in the community. Work may be paid or unpaid; it may involve manual or intellectual labour, including study.

Work provides the opportunity for individuals to contribute to the overall wealth and betterment of society as a whole. Thus work is the key to building a just society. It is the way we contribute to the common good.

Human dignity must be protected and enhanced through the employment or work process. If the dignity of work and by extension the dignity of man is to be protected then the basic rights of workers must be respected and protected. Underlying this is the proposition that work is for man and not man for work. Work and the economy must serve people, not the other way around. The principle that workers ought not to be treated as disposable means to a profitable end but rather as people of intrinsic worth is central to Catholic social teaching.

Pope John XXIII described the true goal of the nation's economy as the personal development of its citizens, guaranteed by a just and proper distribution of a nation's wealth.[96] As such human labour is actually superior to other elements of economic life.[97]

It follows therefore that workers must be treated fairly by their employers. The dignity of the human person must be respected in the workplace. Working conditions and pay must be fair and just. Workers in return should give "a fair day's work for a fair day's pay". As a consequence any employment agreement must be negotiated fairly and based upon the genuine consent of both parties. The duties and responsibilities of employers and employees are closely inter-connected.

Pope John Paul II asserted that labour has a priority over capital and that workers must be treated justly. He also asserted that wages must be sufficient to support a family.[98] Implicit in this is that workers must be able to balance their work and family responsibilities through fair rostering arrangements. They must also be able to rest from work.

Pope Pius XI required that working people should be sufficiently supplied with the fruits of their labour.[99]

The Second Vatican Council declared that people are "the source, the centre and the purpose of all socio-economic life".[100] To achieve work all men and women must have access to employment without discrimination. "A society in which this right [to work] is systematically denied, in which economic policies do not allow workers to reach satisfactory levels of employment, cannot be justified from an ethical point of view, nor can that society obtain social peace." [101]

Taking away from working people the right to protection from unfair dismissal greatly increases job insecurity and undermines the principle of a person's right to work. In such circumstances they cannot be confident they can continue to provide for themselves and their dependants.

As work delivers benefits to both individuals and society as a whole it follows that a key role of government is to do whatever possible to ensure all individuals have access to work that allows them to maximise their intrinsic talents. It is a duty of government and society to endeavour to find suitable employment for all.[102]

The role of government is to assist workers to obtain employment and to provide them with sufficient financial support when they are unable to do so. Elimination of unemployment must be a key goal of government but this must also be balanced by government ensuring that workers have fair pay and conditions and sufficient time free from work for leisure recreation and religious observance. Unemployed people should be treated with respect.[103]

In order to obtain work people often need to acquire skills. It is a key role of government to ensure that all people have the opportunity to acquire skills which will enable them to have fulfilling work opportunities. Individuals also have a responsibility to do what they can to obtain the skills required for employment. Government should invest in education and training. It should also provide financial support where necessary to ensure that people are not deprived of the opportunity to acquire skills because they cannot afford to do so.

Individuals also need to be realistic about the work they are competent to carry out. It is not reasonable for a person to refuse work on the basis that it is "below" their expectation level if that is the only work available. Within reason however people must be free to choose their work.

The right to work however is not an unfettered absolute right as some other rights are, such as the right to life. The right to work is dependent upon work being available.

Among other things this will depend upon where people live. Situations will arise where some people cannot find work because there is no work available or because they do not have the skills to do the work which is available.

Many people in Australia are unable to find paid work, no matter how hard they try. Unemployment deprives people of income and damages their spirit and their sense of self-worth. It damages human dignity.

Sometimes restrictions on the availability of work can occur quite justly. For example, if an employer refuses to provide fair pay and conditions or to discuss legitimate grievances with workers, then the workers may withdraw their labour, that is, go on strike.

Work does not have to be paid work to be legitimate. For example, some families choose to have one parent stay at home full-time to care for children or older relatives. Such people who stay at home, while not usually paid, undertake real work. Indeed it may be argued that there is no more important job than raising the next generation.

Also some people carry out unpaid jobs in the community. This is normally voluntary, often by older or retired people. The work they do in organisations such as St Vincent de Paul is critical to the effective functioning of society.

In October 2000 the Australian Bureau of Statistics reported that on its calculations the value of unpaid work to the Australian economy was $237 billion. Women contributed 65 per cent of this figure. In any consideration the value of unpaid work to the economy is substantial.

Work fulfils fundamental goals of individuals and society. The right to work is therefore critical to the effective functioning of society.

Chapter 14

THE RIGHT TO PERSONAL OWNERSHIP, USE AND DISPOSAL OF PROPERTY, SUBJECT TO THE RIGHT OF OTHERS

Brian J. Coman

While the general principles behind Christian social teaching regarding the right to personal ownership reach back through the centuries of the Christian tradition in the West, their modern development owes much to the great encyclical *Rerum Novarum*, of Pope Leo XIII. At the very end of the nineteenth century, continuing wretched conditions for the ordinary worker in the industrialised West had led to an upsurge of interest in radical socialism. The vast changes wrought by the industrial revolution over the preceding century had led to an altogether new set of social conditions. Hence the title of the Pontiff's great encyclical – literally "On New Things". Here the Church had to steer a course between the injustices of unbridled capitalism and forms of socialism which would reduce the human person to a mere functionary in an all-powerful State. As the encyclical pointed out, "man precedes the State, and possesses, prior to the formation of any State, the right of providing for the substance of his body".

At the same time, while Man may precede the State, he does have obligations to others – to his family, his community, and his country. The situation has been nicely summarised by the Australian poet Mary Gilmore, in these lines from her poem "Nationality":

> All men at God's round table sit
> All men must be fed;
> But this loaf in my hand,
> This is my son's bread.

In the first place, the obligation to share material goods can be seen as a manifestation of the principle of solidarity. But the common good is always oriented towards the progress of individual persons, not of collectivities. There is, in other words, a hierarchy of duty in this regard.

What are the sources of Christian social teaching regarding the right to personal ownership of goods? They arise both from the exercise of human reason and from Divine revelation. Since the time of Aristotle, and probably long before, human reason has recognised that each human life aspires toward some "goal" or "end" – a *telos*, to use the Greek word. The present-day philosopher Alisdair McIntyre puts it thus:

> Within the teleological scheme there is a fundamental contrast between man-as-he-happens-to-be and man-as-he-could-be-if-he-realised-his-essential-nature. Ethics is the science which is to enable men to understand how they make the transition from the former state to the latter.

Such a view is also backed up by both history and common human experience. It is immediately obvious that, for such realisation, some form of private ownership of goods will be necessary. A minimum of food, clothing, tools of trade, etc. is required for the proper functioning of the human person and for the attainment of the proper "end" of human existence. As *Rerum Novarum* states:

> With reason, then, the common opinion of mankind … has found in the careful study of nature, and in the laws of nature, the foundations of the division of property, and the practice of all ages has consecrated

the principle of private ownership, as being pre-eminently in conformity with human nature ...[104]

As an example, it is difficult to imagine St Joseph working with borrowed carpenter's tools or sharing equipment in a carpenter's commune!

But for Aristotle and the early Greeks in general, the notion of equality of human persons was poorly developed. The slave, for instance, was simply "a living tool" for Aristotle, and his or her ends were not considered. The slave was not a *person*, in short. What Christianity brought to this teleological or "ends-based" idea of human life was a proper estimation of the dignity of the individual human person. To quote from the *Catechism of the Catholic Church* (Australian edition):

> Respect for the human person entails respect for the rights that flow from his dignity as a creature. These rights are prior to society and must be recognized by it ... Created in the image of the one God and equally endowed with rational souls, all men have the same nature and the same origin. Redeemed by the sacrifice of Christ, all are called to participate in the same divine beatitude: all therefore enjoy an equal dignity (pars. 1930 and 1934).

When the *Catechism* speaks of the human person as having a *rational* soul, what does this mean? It means that we, unique amongst the created order, have the power of *reason*. This, in turn, entails the notion of objective truth – that we can, by use of our reason, come to formulate general concepts which hold true for all of humanity and are not merely the product of a wholly subjective analysis. It is necessary that this point is emphasised because today, many philosophers and sociologists contend that there is no such thing as objective truth. But without objective truth, there can be no solid basis for what we call "rights". These rights, in the final analysis, depend upon the notion of an objective truth which stands above and outside the mind of the individual.

Another source of Christian social teaching in respect of private ownership of goods can be found by a careful analysis of the Seventh Commandment. It is much more than a command not to steal. It directly implies that, for the sake of the common good, we must respect the right to private property whilst at the same time respecting the "universal destination of goods".[105] By the term "universal destination of goods" we mean that the goods of creation are destined for the whole of humanity. Thus, each person should regard the external goods he or she owns not as personally exclusive, but common to others also in the sense that they can benefit others as well as the legitimate owner.[106] This is why we append to the notion of personal ownership, the proviso that such a right is subject to a consideration of the right of others.

It is also very important to note that the right to personal ownership of property promotes a *personalist*, not an *individualist* mentality. By this we mean that the rights of the individual stem not from the classic liberal perspective of people like J.S. Mill, but from a consideration of that human dignity arising from that perception given in the quotation above from the *Catechism of the Catholic Church*. Thus, personalism implies a certain "solidarist" conception of the individual's responsibility to and for the society around him or her. By "solidarist", we mean a form of friendship or "social charity" which arises directly from a consideration of Christian equality – everyone should look upon his or her neighbour as "another self" endowed with the same hopes, and the same dignity which we would claim for ourselves.[107] When individual freedom is more or less unlimited and takes little account of others, as in the ideas of J.S. Mill, the advantage always goes to the strongest.

The Christian teaching on the right to private property thus falls outside both a strict socialist view and a strict capitalist view. Strict socialism, which would reduce all members of civil society to one level, flies in the face of reason for, as *Rerum Novarum* states:

> There naturally exist among mankind manifold differences of the most important kind; people differ in capacity, skill, health, strength; and unequal fortune

is a necessary result of unequal condition. Such inequality is far from being disadvantageous either to individuals or to the community. Social and public life can only be maintained by means of various kinds of capacity for business and the playing of many parts; and each man, as a rule, chooses the part which suits his own peculiar domestic condition.

On the other hand, unfettered capitalism, which bids fair to reduce the whole of human existence to the pursuit of money and goods, ignores the Christian duty of charity. We have it from Scripture itself that it is more blessed to give than to receive (Acts 20:35) and we are assured that Christ will count a kindness done or refused to the poor as done or refused to Himself (Matthew 25:40).

It is worth pointing out, in conclusion, that the above considerations are by no means restricted to a Christian view of what it means to be human. Article 17 of the Universal Declaration of Human Rights states that "everyone has the right to own property alone as well as in association with others." The Declaration also insists that every person has an obligation to help the needy – "Everyone has duties to the community in which alone the free and full development of his personality is possible. In the exercise of his rights and freedoms, everyone shall be subject only to such limitations as are determined by law solely for the purpose of securing due recognition and respect for the rights and freedoms of others and of meeting the *just requirements of morality, public order and the general welfare* in a democratic society" (my emphasis).[108]

Chapter 15

THE RIGHT TO A LIVING WAGE

Garrick Small

The economic question of wages usually ignores the more fundamental question of their purpose, which is the support of life. If a person has a right to anything, it is the right to life, and from this right comes the social obligation upon people to neither exploit nor extinguish the life of another. The right to life lies behind several of the rights mentioned in the United Nations Universal Declaration of Human Rights, not just article 23, sec. 3 which outlines the right of all people to wages suitable to provide "himself and his family an existence worthy of human dignity". They also lie behind much of the moral teaching of the Catholic Church, from its rejection of the various forms of murder, such as abortion and euthanasia, to its call for a living wage.

Pope Leo XIII was the first to articulate the dimensions of the living wage for the modern world in his 1891 encyclical *Rerum Novarum*. It was developed and expounded by leading Catholic writers, especially Fr John Ryan[109] and the likes of G.K. Chesterton. Methodologically the Pope was applying the consistent position of the Church as found in the economic thought of St Thomas Aquinas and Christian practice back to biblical times. This meant that *Rerum Novarum* used a realist metaphysics to ground fundamental moral deductions regarding key economic questions.

St Thomas dealt with three major economic institutions: property, price and money. From these came three fundamental moral determinations: that property should be privately owned while its use should remain common; that prices should be just; and that usury, the extraction of an income from the mere fact of a loan, was immoral. The matter of just wages relates to just pricing, but in *Rerum Novarum* Pope Leo recognised the necessity of dealing with all three. Rupert Ederer[110] showed how these themes have been consistently carried through all of the social encyclicals, despite their rejection by contemporary economic culture.

To understand prices as moral, one must first appreciate the meaning and power of the concept of morality. A moral is a principle for appropriate relations between intelligent beings. It connotes the exercise of free will. In practice, it always means the free adoption of a course of action that is not in the immediate best interests of the moral actor. This implies that the moral actor has the power and inclination to do otherwise. There is no point in exploring the morality of murder if no one felt inclined, or had the capacity, to kill an innocent person in cold blood. The questions of property, price and usury are moral questions because in the practical order of things, they are situations where moral actors have the power and inclination to violate just relations with others.

Many of the objections to the just wage derive from methodological differences that have been adopted in recent economic thought. Modern economics is grounded in David Hume's rejection of metaphysics and its consequent denial of an objectivist moral philosophy. Like Hume's empiricism, its premises are problematic and its conclusions are provisional, particular, and usually debatable. However, it supports a commercial world that in turn supports it.

Market economics likes to assume key metaphysical premises, and on that basis conclude that economics has no moral content. The market assumed by economic theory is a forum where there are many equal participants who are motivated only by personal utility maximisation, can freely and indifferently enter or leave the market and have perfect knowledge of all aspects of the situation. In such a forum the environment itself forces fair play because no one can be taken advantage of and no one has a life-and-death interest in the outcome. This sort of market might be best represented by wealthy speculators in the stock market who buy and sell using investment funds, excess to their real subsistence needs, in order to gain a profit advantage. No one seriously argues that it is the market form of common transactions, and it would be especially naïve to suggest that it suits the market for labour.

The sale of labour is unlike the sale of most other things. A person usually sells labour out of the need to live, in an environment where the opportunity to directly meet the needs of life is either absent or insufficient. An Aboriginal person living on traditional land in the traditional way does not sell labour to live, but an urban white person usually does. Employers are ultimately persons who have relatively substantial property. This leaves the person selling labour relatively disempowered since the latter's life depends upon the sale.

By contrast, Carlo Panico found, consistent with St Thomas, that the return on capital, or property, is ultimately merely conventional.[111] Contemporary capital asset pricing theory links all financial returns, both equity and property, to the risk-free interest rate, which when adjusted for inflation can be argued to be largely of the nature of usury. Usury today is an inflammatory term, but Pope Leo XIII used it accurately to describe the problem of wages as having been "increased by rapacious usury, which, although more than once condemned by the Church, is nevertheless, under a different guise, but with like injustice, still practiced by covetous and grasping men."[112]

The question of wages is therefore really the question of the balance between the return to labour and the return to property and capital. The data has shown that over the long term wages rates have not fared well compared to property and stock prices. In the period 1970 to 2006 Australian urban land prices lagged behind stock market growth but still rose in excess of wages to the extent that whereas a single average family income could purchase a cottage in 1970, it now requires two incomes to buy a mere strata apartment.

During the same time working hours have generally increased while industrial relations structures maintaining wages have been eroded.[113]

This evidence runs counter to the theory Thomas Woods posited when he criticised the social encyclicals for what he considered their uninformed criticism of economics.[114] While Woods' complaint with Catholic social thought is deficient in many respects, its best test is perhaps the positive evidence, which after all is the supposed methodological base of his economics. Woods' only credible argument is that the payment of a wage above that formed in a market unrestrained by moral or legal imperatives would disadvantage workers, principally by pricing workers out of the labour market.

This argument is valid only if one takes a short view. For a particular firm, in a particular period, the imposition of a higher wage will cause unemployment, only if the firm has a labour-substitution strategy available or it is unwilling to lower its profitability to maintain its productivity. When Henry Ford raised wages for his employees, merely because he wanted them to be able to afford the cars that they were producing, his moral choice must have injured his personal profits. This supposed economic foolishness did not cause unemployment or Henry to go out of business. Rather, it attracted the best workers and forced his competitors to similarly raise their wages in a spiral that stimulated consumption, and eventually Ford's profitability skyrocketed, along with benefits for the whole community.[115]

The meaner approach is to use labour substitutes as an industrial weapon. Contrary to one of Woods' claims, when un-Christian businessmen obtain labour-replacing technology, the result is lower wages, and elevated unemployment. While this is implicit in the West over the last generation, Fred Harrison is representative of economic historians who recognised it as the dominant gambit through the Industrial Revolution.[116] He further identified the ultimate beneficiaries as mainly the landowners.

The other way unemployment can result is to search for cheaper labour and it has been a characteristic of capitalism since the fifteenth century, first by immoral guildsmen, and later by colonists using indigenous or indentured labour. It continues today in the transfer of productive capital to low-cost locations such as China. However, this decision is simply the rejection of the moral imperative, not its result. It does demonstrate that the living wage requires a moral will to be adopted by the majority of the community, especially by the majority of the employer community. It means the exercise of a different type of freedom, the one Pope John Paul II clearly articulated as becoming of a Christian in *Veritatis Splendor*. The reformation was largely about rejecting a life ordered by that sort of freedom and it is no coincidence that rejection of Catholicism ushered in modern capitalism.

Thorold Rogers, though no friend of the Catholic Church, found that the fortunes of English working people were decimated by that transition. In the Catholic centuries from 1100 to 1300 wages rose by somewhere between five to eight times, but in the century of the reformation they fell by over 60 per cent. The slide was not halted until the mid-nineteenth century.[117] It is salutary to recall that Australia was first populated by victims of free market wages policy – working-class citizens of the greatest commercial power of the time who were reduced to stealing to provide for their families.

The threat of socialism and the organisation of labour have been the major drivers in returning wages to reasonable levels over the last two centuries. These motivated nineteenth-century British Tory Prime Minister Benjamin Disraeli and conservative German Chancellor Otto von Bismarck to enact labour laws that had the effect of strengthening wages. No serious economic historian would hold that these moves disadvantaged labour.

The twentieth century has been more complex, but the pattern tends to be the same. Generally the political threat of organised labour has been successful and its sober application, through organs such as the Australian Labor Party, has been successful in gaining a sound level of wages, at least up to about the 1960s. It is no accident that the best of Catholic political talent were associated with that party over the same period. History supports the living wage.

Despite the evidence, we live in an era where market economists disagree furiously amongst themselves about most economic issues, but combine only to decry the promotion of genuine solidarity befitting the human person. St Bonaventure prefaced his treatment of the economic question with the observation, "If one does not love one's neighbour, it is not easy to do him justice".[118] Willing just wages for our neighbour will not be the result of impersonal market forces, but the result of a higher sentiment and one that has long been recognised as the hallmark of the Christian. Despite the protestations of theoretical economists, it works. Unfortunately it will not work unless Pope Leo's most salient insight is also upheld: "if human society is to be healed now, in no other way can it be healed save by a return to Christian life and Christian institutions" (*Rerum Novarum* n. 27).

Chapter 16

THE RIGHT TO COLLECTIVE BARGAINING

Keith Harvey

In 2006, Bishop Manning of Parramatta declared: "The right of workers to act *collectively* is central to Catholic social teaching."[119] While this is true, there is no specific reference to collective *bargaining* as such in Leo XIII's 1891 encyclical *Rerum Novarum* nor in the *Compendium of the Social Doctrine of the Church* released a century later by Pope John Paul II.

In the first case, this is not surprising, since the term did not exist in 1891. It was coined in 1898 by the English Socialist Beatrice Webb, who with her husband published two seminal works on trade unionism and industrial relations in the 1890s.[120] As defined by them, collective bargaining was a means of achieving an essential protection for workers – which they called the "Common Rule": that is, wages and conditions applying to "whole bodies of workers" in a particular trade or industry. The Webbs wrote that the "device of common rule" was a "universal feature of Trade Unionism" utilised by unions everywhere. Without it, wages and conditions would be subject to so-called free competition arrived at by individual bargaining between parties of very unequal bargaining strength.[121]

Common rule, as a means of securing legally binding collectively bargained outcomes, played an important role in Australian industrial law and practice for 100 years. It remains fundamental to an attempt to equalise the bargaining power of workers with that of employers. As Paul VI wrote in *Populorum Progressio*, in the context of justice between countries: "The teaching of Leo XIII is always valid: if the positions of the contracting parties are too unequal, the consent of the parties does not suffice to guarantee the justice of their contract …"[122]

Catholic social teaching therefore emphasises collectivity, and collective bargaining flows inevitably from this fundamental principle and other aspects of social teaching about work. These other dimensions include the dignity and the communal vocation of the human person, participation, solidarity, equality, love of neighbour and, of course, the right of free association.

While collective bargaining is most commonly thought of in the context of industrial relations, it has other applications as well. Small businesses and independent producers such as farmers can band together to deal with larger businesses, including manufacturers and retail outlets. This is specifically allowed and promoted under the Australian Trade Practices Act and can be an important tool in achieving economic justice for smaller enterprises and primary producers.

In the industrial relations context, the right to form and join employee associations has been upheld in all the social encyclicals since *Rerum Novarum*. Leo XIII noted specifically that Unions "exist of their own right"[123] and, as a result, have the right to determine how they should organise their affairs in the best interests of the workers they represent.

Pope Leo noted: "The consciousness of his own weakness urges man to call in aid from without. We read in the pages of the holy writ: 'It is better that two should be together than one; for they have the advantage of their society'…"[124] In the New American Bible, this text reads: "Two are better than one: they get a good wage for their labor."

The encyclicals and other teaching documents of the Church also emphasise the right of workers to fair wages and conditions, and especially wages that meet the living needs of the worker and the worker's family. Collective action was essential to achieve these outcomes. The right to strike, under certain conditions, was justifiable.

Of course, with the right and power of collective action comes responsibility: successive Popes have warned of the need to ensure that collective action is always directed towards the common good and not for other purposes, such as class struggle for its own sake or for purely political purposes.[125] The misuse of collective power for other purposes lessens support for unions from members and the general public and leaves it vulnerable to attack from hostile forces.

That the Church went as far as it did in support of collective action in 1891 was remarkable since largely, outside of England, unions and industrial action remained illegal in many European countries and in the USA until late in the nineteenth century. Unions were legalised in France only in 1884 and "combinations" of workers to raise wages by collective action were frequently treated as conspiracies against the natural economic order, and suppressed.

Trade unions have generally sought to achieve collective outcomes in particular workplaces, industries and occupations. For most workers, individual bargaining and agreements almost inevitably mean "unequal treaties" favouring the employer (although in limited circumstances individual workers with skills and expertise in demand can bargain successfully).

At the time *Rerum Novarum* was written, collective action, including the resort to strike action, was the only means at the disposal of ordinary workers acting in union to achieve the goal of a common outcome.

Some Catholic social thinkers in Europe at the time were beginning to think of alternative means of resolving disputes and fixing wages and conditions, including arbitration.[126] During the 1880s in Australia the expanding union movement attempted to assert common wages and conditions for employees in the maritime and pastoral industries. When the employers resisted, the workers struck, and despite protracted disputes, their actions were defeated.

A Royal Commission into the strikes concluded shortly after *Rerum Novarum* was published and the Commission's report summarised Pope Leo's teachings. Australia's great Catholic spokesperson for the rights of workers, Cardinal Moran, spoke publicly about these issues in Sydney in August 1891.

The Cardinal attacked "freedom of contract" – a key issue in the strikes – by which employers meant freedom to employ non-union workers. The Cardinal declared that these words had been turned into "an engine of robbery ... a mockery, a delusion and a snare" the result of which was starvation wages because "when one party to a contract can impose and the other party to it must accept its terms, however burdensome", the outcome is unjust.[127]

Since collective action had failed, the Cardinal suggested that "the friends of labour should promote boards of conciliation and arbitration".[128] Arbitration was gaining support from other quarters as well, since even where bargaining was successful, there was no legal impediment to either side walking away from a deal once made.[129]

Australia took the Cardinal at his word, opting for systems of conciliation and arbitration in the colonies immediately prior to Federation and in the new Commonwealth after 1901. The new Arbitration Court was given the power to make its awards common rule. The influence of Catholic social teaching on the development of this almost unique Australian measure has been noted.[130]

The new Australian system was not designed to replace collective bargaining but to provide access to arbitration when direct bargaining failed. However, arbitration quickly became the preferred course for many unions, while employers resisted the imposition on them of court-determined wages and conditions which took account of social needs. Collective bargaining was never completely subsumed by arbitration – since bargaining about "over award" payments continued, site- and employer-specific agreements abounded and industrial tribunals often only implemented new conditions after they had been won "on the ground" by direct collective action.

However, in Australia, Catholic social teaching has been often more concerned with issues such as the living wage than with access to collective bargaining rights, which were less important here than in other industrial systems.

Nevertheless, the Church's social teachings continued to support the right of workers to collectively bargain by implication and explicitly. In the English translation of *Mater et Magistra,* John XXIII specifically referred to the development of unions "for the specific purpose of co-operation, in particular by means of collective bargaining", and noted "how timely and imperative it is that the workers exert their influence".[131]

The Church has also explicitly supported the work of the International Labour Organization[132], a specialised agency of the UN which sets core labour standards including Conventions on the Right to Organise and Collectively Bargain as being fundamental to worker rights.[133]

When John Paul II visited Australian in 1986 he remarked favourably on Australia's industrial relations system:

> Australia has a long and proud history of settling industrial disputes and promoting cooperation by its almost unique system of arbitration and conciliation. Over the years this system has helped to defend the rights of workers and promote their well being, while at the same time taking into account the needs and the future of the whole community.[134]

This Australian system lasted for 90 years until the early 1990s, but has since changed dramatically. In 1993, a Labor government formally re-introduced collective bargaining as a legal supplement to industrial awards. Employers and workers could make agreements which had the force of law and overrode awards, under certain conditions.

In 1996 and 2005, new laws allowed individual employee agreements, which now take precedence over all other forms of agreement. The driving forces behind the legislation are now individualism, the "free market" and globalization. The economic imperative, not social concerns, now appears central to workplace laws.

This chapter is not a commentary on Australia's industrial legislation but a reflection on the principle of collective bargaining and how it has been applied in Australia. Values central to Catholic social teaching and the collective interests of workers have greatly diminished in importance in recent times.

In his 2006 Encyclical Letter, Benedict XVI wrote of "the unbreakable bond between love of God and love of neighbour"[135]. A collective approach to industrial relations combines regard for one another with the common good and justice for all.

Industrial relations law speaks about the values underpinning society. Catholic social teaching applies divine law to human societies. Australian industrial laws traditionally sought socially just outcomes, achieved in part through respect for the right of workers to organise collectively within a framework of law and the public interest.

This country responded to the circumstances of its own history, international trends and thinking as well as, consciously or unconsciously, Catholic social teaching on this issue dating back to the first social encyclical and beyond. Collective bargaining remains fundamental to the rights of workers to ensure that justice and the common good prevail.

Chapter 17

THE RIGHT TO ASSOCIATE BY INDUSTRIES AND PROFESSIONS TO ACHIEVE ECONOMIC JUSTICE

Henrik Jurisevic[136]

The publication of Pope Leo XIII's encyclical *Rerum Novarum*[137] in 1891 developed the principle of workers' rights to associate in order to achieve economic justice. If, by economic justice, we mean wages and conditions which allow a worker to live a decent life by providing the basic necessities of life for themselves and their dependants, then the right to associate is a right which stands on its own. This discussion explores what is entailed in the right to associate for industriy and workers as professionals and what justice in an economic sense may mean for industry and professional workers.

We have rights that are given to us (and also taken away) by society, and those that flow to us by virtue of being human. The former carry with them responsibilities and obligations to society. The latter do not – we do not have to demonstrate that we deserve them and they cannot be taken away.[138] These distinctions do not mean that these rights are mutually exclusive.

For society to function with purpose, we need a wide variety of callings with each individual or group playing its part and making a contribution for the benefit of itself and of society. It is not a matter of an individual or group being more important than another. In seeking to achieve these aims, it is natural for citizens to form associations, for as *Rerum Novarum* tells us, "The consciousness of his own weakness urges man to call in aid from without".[139] We are stronger as a group than we are as individuals. Streek and Schmitter argue that "'association' or 'interest group,' and most particularly occupational association, must be added to state, market, and community as the fourth basic source of social order." [140]

An industry or professional association provides a forum for its members to share information and discuss topics of mutual interest. It seeks to promote the interests of its members in terms which allow its members to prosper, including in an economic sense. An association also presents a united front in representing the interests of its members in negotiations with government and other organisations, and in making representations to government about policy and legislation which may affect its members' interests. An association also has the means to represent its members' interests in a way that individual members may not have.

According to *Rerum Novarum*, justice must be "*distributive – toward each and every class alike*"[141] (italics in original). Distributive justice, as John Rawls points out, also relies on justice in our basic social institutions, which, necessarily, includes the process that is followed to achieve it.[142]

To briefly explore the way in which industries may associate to achieve economic justice, we will consider two examples which have the process of justice at their centre. As the following examples will show, the very fact that industry associations participate in, and contribute to, the justice process in terms of representing their members is an affirmation of their right to do so.

The first example is the case where a local chamber of commerce makes representations to a local government authority on behalf of the local business proprietors who are concerned about a proposed course of action by the authority. In this case, justice requires that the concerns of the local business proprietors be treated with respect and taken into account by the local government authority in making its decisions, which must be in the public interest.

The second, more complex, example is much broader in scope and takes its lead from *Rerum Novarum*, which recognises that consideration must be given to the rights and duties of employers as well as the rights and duties of the workers.[143] An industry association may represent the interests of its members, where its members are employers, in the area of industrial relations dealing with the determination of wages by a statutory body. The parties to such a determination may include representatives from unions, various tiers of government, religious associations, and industry associations, among others. In making its decisions in these cases, the statutory body typically hears submissions from the parties and also considers factors such as the Australian economy, the relevant State economy, the wage environment, and the various effects of their decision.

What does justice require in a case such as this? First, justice requires seeking a decision from an independent body which carefully considers a broad range of factors before making its decision. Next, the process must provide the parties with an opportunity to argue their case on behalf of those they represent. In addition, justice requires that the body's decision represents the public interest. What these two examples have in common is that justice entails the right to be represented, the right to a fair hearing, and an outcome from the justice process that stands for the common good.

Professional workers in our society have authority and discretion to an extent that is not always available to workers outside the professions. They are also in a position of trust, a characteristic that is fundamental to a profession, which could also be considered to be the foundation of a profession's authority and discretion. Indeed, Koehn argues that what is truly distinctive about the professions is their moral commitment to serve an instrinsic good.[144] Regardless of this, the professions are not free from criticism.[145] Freidson contends that, in defending themselves from criticism, the professions must prepare an argument that "confronts and explains" the claim that the core of professional institutions is economic privilege which is based on attaining prescribed credentials and on exercising a monopoly over who can perform certain types of work in the marketplace.[146]

Monopoly and credentialism[147] need to be taken seriously, as Freidson does in comprehensively answering these criticisms.[148] There are very good reasons why certain types of work must only be performed by persons with particular qualifications, experience and skill. That is, the nature of the work itself *genuinely* demands it. However, in some cases it can be difficult to identify, define and reach agreement on where the nature of the work does genuinely demand it.

In considering the manner in which professional workers may associate to achieve economic justice, there are two categories of interest to us. The first is the professional worker who is a salaried employee of either an organisation in private practice or the state. The second category is the professional who is a member of a professional association, whether by statute or by choice, where membership is of direct economic benefit. Professionals may also be in both categories. Again, as discussed earlier with respect to industry, the fact that professional workers do associate in these ways is an affirmation of their right to do so.

In the case of salaried professional workers, their salary and conditions may be expressed by, for example, an enterprise agreement or an award resulting from negotiations between an association that represents their profession and either an employer association or a single employer.[149] Agreements and awards are multifaceted instruments which recognize the wage relativities that exist within skill-based career structures (based on factors such as the qualifications, skill, experience, and the level of responsibility of the person performing the work). Maintaining wage relativities and adjustments for increases in the cost of living represents an important economic benefit, but another element is also included. It is an element that is integral to a profession and to the profession's role in society. It is professional ethics.

The second category of professional workers derive economic benefit from membership of a professional association because people who use their services have confidence in dealing with them because they are members. Before a professional association can reach this point, it needs to establish itself as being a credible and effective entity that can be taken seriously. To achieve credibility, a professional association needs to demonstrate that it stands not just for the advantage of its members (economic or otherwise), but that it exists within an ethical framework which is compatible with, and of service to, the society in which its members work.

A professional association has an obligation to accredit applicants so that only those with the prescribed qualifications and experience are admitted to membership. Following this, it needs to develop and implement a policy for continuing professional development which demonstrates its members' commitment to maintaining their competence to practice. The professional association also has a responsibility to deal justly with complaints made against its members, and to discipline members if necessary. Finally, the development of a code of ethics is essential, as is promoting awareness of the code among its members and assisting members to understand it so that they are encouraged in putting it into practice.[150] All of this appears to be fairly straightforward when stated like this. It is not. Professional ethics is hard work. It goes beyond codes of ethics, which cannot be expected to do the job alone. As Coady says, it requires moral deliberation on the part of the professional worker.[151] It gives professional workers and professional associations cause for reflection.

Chapter 18

THE RIGHT TO ASSISTANCE FROM SOCIETY, IF NECESSARY FROM THE STATE, IN DISTRESS OF PERSON OR FAMILY

Catherine Althaus

The parable of the Good Samaritan, the plight of babies and the frail and aged shout to us of the right of human beings in distress to obtain assistance from society. Humans are vulnerable and often stand isolated, unprotected and in severe need of help. The principles of human dignity, solidarity and subsidiarity demand that Catholics provide such help.

The first principle of all social organisation is that "it must serve the human person, made in God's image and likeness"[152]. Having the human person as the end and purpose of all social organisation is a fundamental principle that must neither be violated nor taken away.

Human beings are of course social by nature in that their development derives from living together with others[153]. A human being can survive in isolation – if circumstances demand or they have the temperament and freely choose to do so, say in a hermitic lifestyle – but they do not thrive under such conditions. On the contrary, human beings "have potentialities which remain undeveloped if they live in isolation"[154]. According to *Gaudium et Spes*, "The social nature of man shows that there is an interdependence between personal betterment and the improvement of society. Man by his very nature stands in need of life in society…"[155]

The first society is the family, followed by the associations formed in civic society and lastly the society achieved through political means through the state. All of these societal forms require application of solidarity, which enables human beings to acknowledge and put into action the belief that there is a transcendent dimension to humanity; a power above to which we are subject which places restraints upon human selfishness in order to achieve healthy, happy, fruitful and purposeful living. As it is put in *Libertatis Conscientia*,[156] "Solidarity is the direct requirement of human and supernatural brotherhood". The principle of solidarity is not a Christian insight but one shared by believers of different faiths as well as non-believers, even if there is not always agreement on how people should work in society to see solidarity become a reality.

A third principle structuring all social organisation is that of subsidiarity, a term from the Latin *subsidium* which means "help"[157]. Subsidiarity advocates that the level of organisation that is best suited to meet the needs of those in distress is the level that should provide the assistance. There is a sort of "flowing chain of assistance or support" – something like the ripples flowing outwards from a stone thrown in a pond – where the links between the chains must be respected. As the levels of society spread outwards, those organizations of society must not impede or attempt to take over the responsibilities of those closer to the distressed. Families should not attempt to take away the freedom of individual human beings, civic societies should not attempt to assume the roles and responsibilities of families, and the state should not impede the roles and responsibilities of civic associations. According to *Quadragesimo Anno*:

> It is an injustice and at the same time a great evil and disturbance of right order to assign to a greater and higher association what lesser and subordinate organisations can do. For every social activity ought of its very nature to furnish help to the members of the body social, and never destroy or absorb them.[158]

And the help given and the manner in which it is given should "have the aim of making those who receive the help independent again as soon as possible"[159]. The pillar of human dignity demands that human beings be given their freedom – defined not as a self-serving, licentious, do-whatever-you-like freedom but as freedom under the natural and divine laws. Assistance, in other words, does not equate with dependence, as this would violate human dignity and cause decay not only to the human person themselves but also to the societies of which they are a part[160].

The tenets of human dignity and solidarity have natural law breeding as much as their origins can be traced from the Old Testament. The obligation of subsidiarity, too, can be seen in the Old Testament law (for example, through the injunctions to succour the widow, the orphan and stranger in need, and in the New Testament parable of the Good Samaritan) even if the term was used first in the encyclical *Quadragesimo Anno* in 1931[161].

The right to assistance from society, therefore, has been promoted throughout the history of the Church. Its development to include the notion of subsidiarity occurred especially as different forms of society emerged and changed. In the early Church an emphasis was especially laid on the assistance to be garnered from other families and civic associations and also from the Church itself. The selection of specially nominated persons as deacons designated to serve the orphans and widows is an example of the attention and dedication that the Church devoted to this particular right (see Acts 6:1-6). Over time, this social charity role has expanded from the *xenodochia* of the early Church[162] to the massive caring arms of organisations such as the St Vincent de Paul Society, Caritas and the numerous Catholic hospitals and schools across the globe that provide health care and education in the community.

Over time, attention has had to be paid to the appropriate role to be played by the state in providing welfare. Today, with the complex array of networked partnerships between community organisations, private sector providers and government, persons and families are being plugged into systems of support that cut across society.

Unemployment, poverty, serious sickness, lack of education and dysfunctionality in human relationships (often expressed in the form of abuse) are all examples of persons and families in distress which call upon the right to assistance. Natural catastrophes also demand the support of societies to aid those in need. The Compendium of the Social Doctrine of the Church[163] devotes special attention to the plight of nations and peoples that suffer on the international level from poverty, the crippling effects of foreign debt, crimes against humanity and the atrocities that create refugees. While there is much yet to be worked out in the establishment of an authentic international society, the Church does signal this as an important societal connection that creates moral obligation and demands careful attention.

Thus the plight of individuals right through the full ambit of families, neighbourhoods, communities, regions, nations and the wider global family is at stake. While Australia overall boasts a high standard of living, it faces the full scale of all these issues. If the Catholic tradition is to be followed, human dignity must be upheld and respected and subsidiarity must be applied so that those in need are given their due freedom and an abusive cycle of dependence is avoided.

In an "everyday sense" each person can apply and promote the right by being alert to the needs of themselves and others. Each person must decide for themselves what they are best placed to do in terms of providing time, practical support, financial assistance, emotional and spiritual encouragement, volunteering contributions, material possessions and the like which will alleviate the suffering and burden of those in distress in order to help them reach their full potential. The Compendium[164] gives some other examples of practical application of the right (e.g. appropriate subsidies for the subsistence of unemployed workers and their families, the right to a pension and to insurance for old age, sickness, and in the case of work-related accidents, as well as the right to social security connected with maternity). Whatever the chosen means or at what level, there are countless ways to identify those in need and provide them with relief that respects their human dignity and helps return them to independence.

The dangers of not applying assistance are well documented; glaring tragedies of poverty, homelessness, unemployment, illness, abuse, deprivation of love, emotional support and self-esteem, racial and gender inequality, recourse to crime.

But over-provision of assistance can also cripple the person in need and damage their dignity as well as the health of the society. *Centesimus Annus* gives one example pertaining to the risks of state intervention:

> The State has the right to intervene when social sectors are too weak ... Such interventions have remedied forms of poverty and deprivation unworthy of a human person. However, excesses and abuses have provoked very harsh criticisms of the welfare state. By depriving civil society of its responsibility, the social assistance state leads to a loss of human energies and to inordinate increase in public agencies accompanied by an enormous increase in spending.[165]

The same can be said for intervention by civic bodies or families who are just as capable of creating or enforcing dependence and stifling human freedom. Families who are too controlling of children and stifle their maturity, voluntary organisations that provide assistance to needy people without encouraging and assisting them to reintegrate into society and regain their independence; all are examples where the right to assistance from society is violated and the associated benefits abrogated and nullified.

We all know the dilemmas in providing assistance. A beggar in the street may benefit from the money of a passer-by, or they might use the money to purchase drugs that will help ensure a cycle of dependence and addiction that injures human dignity. The assessment is complex and sensitive in aggregate but perhaps more easily resolved in the personal calculation. What can I do to help *this* person? If this person is Christ, *what do I choose to do to help?*

For any Catholic, the demands are clear. One must pray and educate oneself in having an informed conscience that will be able to decide the balance of justice and mercy in ensuring each person is given the fullness of their human dignity. One should not violate one's own human dignity in order to help another, but nor must one ignore the lack of human dignity of another when one's own dignity is safe. On the contrary, Christ's call to openness to the personal needs of others demands we each make effort to reach out to those around us. Our ability and willingness to do so with loving discernment marks us as Christians.

Afterword

James Franklin

It is sixty years since the eighteen rights that form the chapter titles of this book were listed by the US National Catholic Welfare Conference. At that time, the catastrophes of 1914 to 1945 weighed heavily on memory and the comparatively happy future was not in view. Nor were many of the concerns of more recent times, such as the environment, feminism and the self-determination of colonial peoples, nor deregulation and economic rationalism.

Nevertheless the list of rights holds up remarkably well as a foundation for thought about the present and future. The countries that have experienced better times since 1947 – Australia among them – are those that have made a fair attempt to implement all those rights. In the countries that are the worst to live in – the North Koreas and Zimbabwes – not one of those rights is secure, and it is exactly the persistent and unpunished violation of those rights that makes those states enemies of their own peoples. We have come to understand, too, that attempts to solve the problems of failed Third World states by purely economic means such as development aid are ineffective or counterproductive while unrestrained kleptocracies continue to rule them: rights are as essential a precondition to economic development as they are to basic human well-being.

In Australia and other constitutional democracies, there is a general framework of respect for rights. A strong and independent legal system and democratic political institutions protect the great majority of people and provide avenues of recourse for those whose rights are abused or threatened. Where problems arise is in the tendency of certain classes of people and certain issues to "fall between the cracks". The shameful revelations of chronic violence in remote aboriginal communities have shown that vulnerable individuals, especially women and children, have been left to the mercy of vicious local tyrants. The wider society sometimes closed its eyes to news of those abuses under the guise of "respect for cultural traditions"; it serves as a reminder that rights are the rights of individuals, and must take precedence where they clash with collectivist cultural practices. Every child, remote or not, has the same right to be born free of fetal alcohol syndrome and then has the right to live in a peaceful home and to be educated in English.

Other groups whose rights have been sometimes overlooked in the crush of self-protective efforts by powerful groups – no doubt related to their difficulties in either suing or voting – include the mentally ill, the frail aged and disabled and their carers, the very young without strong parents, foreign nationals of powerless states, and refugees incarcerated for excessive periods. Until respect for human rights extends to every human being, in the country and out of it, Australia's justified pride in its record cannot be as total as one would wish of a country with its Christian moral heritage.

CONTRIBUTORS

James Franklin is Associate Professor, School of Mathematics and Statistics, UNSW. Author of: *Catholic Values and Australian Realities*, *Corrupting the Youth: A History of Philosophy in Australia* and *The Science of Conjecture: Evidence and Probability Before Pascal*.

John Sharpe co-founded IHS Press, a publisher dedicated exclusively to the social teachings of the Catholic Church. He has re-issued, edited, and annotated works of many of the English writers of the twentieth-century Catholic renaissance, including Hilaire Belloc, G. K. Chesterton, Arthur Penty and Fr Vincent McNabb. Others of his editorial works include annotated editions of Amintore Fanfani's *Catholicism, Protestantism, and Capitalism* and Fr Heinrich Pesch's *Ethics and the National Economy*.

Richard Rymarz has published widely in religious education, theology and on contemporary Catholic culture. He holds the Kule Chair in Catholic Religious Education at St Joseph's College, University of Alberta.

Michael Casey is Private Secretary to Dr George Pell, Catholic Archbishop of Sydney, as well as Permanent Fellow, John Paul II Institute, Melbourne.

Sam Gregg is Director of Research at the Acton Institute, an Adjunct Professor at the Pontifical Lateran University, a consultant for Oxford Analytica Ltd, and general editor of the Lexington Book Series Studies in Ethics and Economics.

Damian Grace is Associate Professor and Postgraduate Coordinator, School of Philosophy, University of New South Wales.

Marita Winters is the Director of the Catholic Enquiry Centre for the Australian Catholic Bishops Conference in Sydney.

Anthony Cleary is the Director of Religious Education and Evangelisation for the Catholic Education Office, Sydney. Prior to this appointment in 2006 he was the Director of the Confraternity of Christian Doctrine (Sydney), which coordinates the religious instruction of some 32,000 Catholic students attending public schools. In this role, Anthony was the General Editor of a catechetical series, *Christ Our Light and Life*, which has sold internationally.

Paul Russell is the Senior Officer for the Office for Family and Life in the Archdiocese of Adelaide. He is a member of the Board of Management of the Southern Cross Bioethics Institute.

Andrew Hamilton SJ is the consulting editor for *Eureka Street*. He also teaches at the United Faculty of Theology in Melbourne.

Brenda Hubber is the Executive Officer of the Melbourne Catholic Migrant and Refugee Office.

Michael Hogan retired in 1997 from the Department of Government at the University of Sydney after 20 years of teaching. He continues there as an Honorary Associate. He edited and published collections of the annual Social Justice Statements of the Australian Catholic Bishops, 1940-1966, *Justice Now!* (1990), and of the Catholic Commission for Justice and Peace, 1973-1987, *Option for the Poor* (1992). In recent years he has written on aspects of New South Wales politics for the celebration of the sesquicentenary of responsible government in that State in 2006. His best known book is probably *The Sectarian Strand: Religion in Australian History* (1987).

Ian Blandthorn is National Assistant Secretary of the Shop Distributive and Allied Employees Association.

Brian Coman a former research biologist, describes himself as a "refugee from the phantasms of science". In his retirement he has taken up studies in the humanities and was recently awarded his second PhD. Brian lectures at La Trobe University, Bendigo. His collection *A Loose Canon* was published by Connor Court in 2007.

Garrick Small is Senior Lecturer, School of the Built Environment, Associate Head of School (Teaching and Learning), School of the Built Environment, University of Technology, Sydney.

Keith Harvey is an employee of the Australian Services Union. He has worked in the Australian trade union movement in a variety of roles for nearly 35 years, but particularly in recent times as an Industrial Officer. He is familiar with Australian industrial law and practice, particularly as it applies to industrial awards and collective bargaining. Keith takes a close interest in labour history and the interplay between Catholic social teaching and industrial relations. He is also interested in vocational education and training for workers and represents unions on a number of organisations promoting skill development. Keith is married with three children and is a parishioner at Holy Family Church, Mount Waverley in Victoria.

Henrik Jurisevic is a civil engineer.

Catherine Althaus (PhD Griffith) is from the Centre for Governance and Public Policy, Griffith University.

ENDNOTES

[1] T. Judt, *Postwar: A history of Europe since 1945* (London, 2005), pp. 501-3.
[2] J. Franklin, "Regulated capitalism, market socialism", *Dissent* 5 (2001), 11-13.
[3] J.O. Urmson, *Aristotle's Ethics* (Oxford, 1988), p. 71.
[4] F.A. Hayek, *Law, Legislation and Liberty:* Vol 2, The Mirage of Social Justice (London, 1976).
[5] D. Stove, *Darwinian Fairytales* (New York, 2006), p. 177.
[6] "The impulse to acquisition ... has in itself nothing to do with capitalism. That impulse exists and has existed among waiters, physicians, coachmen, artists, prostitutes, dishonest officials ... capitalism is identical with the pursuit of profit, and forever *renewed* profit, by means of a continuous, rational, capitalistic enterprise." M. Weber, *The Protestant Ethic and the Spirit of Capitalism*, introduction (London, 2001, pp. xxxi-xxxii).
[7] Hayek, p. 76.
[8] Hayek, p. 73.
[9] R.E. Zupko and R.A. Laures, *Straws in the Wind: Medieval urban environmental law – the case of Northern Italy* (Boulder, 1996).
[10] J. Gordley, *The Philosophical Origins of Modern Contract Doctrine* (Oxford, 1991).
[11] John Paul II, *Centesimus Annus*, 15, 48.
[12] J. Franklin, "Accountancy as computational casuistics", *Eureka Street*, 9 (1) (Jan/Feb, 1999), 2, 43-6; especially with the expansion of compensation law to cover most cases of pure economic loss: T. Carver, "Woolcock Street Investments Pty Ltd v CDG Pty Ltd: beyond *Bryan*: Builders' liability and pure economic loss", *Melbourne University Law Review* 29 (2005), 270-97.
[13] J. Franklin, "Risk-driven global compliance regimes in banking and accounting: the new Law Merchant", *Law, Probability and Risk* 4 (2005), 237-50.
[14] W. Coleman and A. Hagger, *Exasperating Calculators* (Sydney, 2001), ch. 10.
[15] P. Booth, ed, *Catholic Social Teaching and the Market Economy* (London, 2007); D. Villey, "The market economy and Roman Catholic thought", *International Economic Papers* 9 (1959), 93-124.
[16] A. Norton, "Liberalism and social justice: the unhappy couple", in M. Goldsmith, *Social Justice: Fraud or fair go?* (Kingston, ACT, 1998), 21-9.
[17] T.E. Huff, *The Rise of Early Modern Science: Islam, China, and the West* (Cambridge, 1993), ch. 4.
[18] D. Stove, "Santamaria and the bishops", *Honi Soit* 43 (32) (29/10/70), quoted in J. Franklin, *Corrupting the Youth: A history of philosophy in Australia* (Sydney, 2003), pp. 291-2.
[19] P. Costello, "Restoring confidence in corporate morality", *Quadrant* 34 (9) (Sept 1990), 20-22; F. Fukuyama, *Trust: The social virtues and the creation of prosperity* (London, 1995).

[20] M. James, "Markets and morality", in C. James, C. Jones and A. Norton, eds, *A Defence of Economic Rationalism* (Sydney, 1993), 160-7.
[21] Leo XIII, *Rerum Novarum*, 32; discussion in B. Duncan, *The Church's Social Teaching: From Rerum Novarum to 1931* (Melbourne, 1991).
[22] Contrary to some more socialist conceptions of "social justice", as criticised in Goldsmith, *Social Justice: Fraud or fair go?*; various suggestions in Catholic Bishops of Australia, *Common Wealth and Common Good: A statement on wealth distribution* (Melbourne, 1991).
[23] K. Blackburn, "The living wage in Australia: a secularization of Catholic ethics on wages", 1891-1907, *Journal of Religious History* 20 (1996), 93-113.
[24] R. Gaita, *Good and Evil: An absolute conception* (2nd ed, Abingdon, 2004), p. 315.
[25] John Paul II, "Message on the Occasion of the International Symposium on the Dignity and Rights of the Mentally Disabled Person", 2004, http://www.vatican.va/holy_father/john_paul_ii/speeches/2004/january/documents/hf_jp-ii_spe_20040108_handicap-mentale_en.html
[26] *Catechism of the Catholic Church*, par. 2267.
[27] *Rerum Novarum*, 14.
[28] J. Bernardin, Address: Consistent Ethic of Life Conference, 1986, http://www.priestsforlife.org/magisterium/bernardinportland.html
[29] Elsewhere he notes that "since the end of society is to make men better, the chief good that society can possess is virtue." (*Rerum Novarum*, 34).
[30] See, for instance, Jeremiah Newman (Professor of Sociology at St Patrick's College, Maynooth, Ireland), *Studies in Political Morality* (Dublin, 1963); Derek Cross, "Tolerance as Catholic doctrine", *First Things*, October 1992, pp. 38-44; and Michael Davies, *The Second Vatican Council and Religious Liberty* (Long Prairie, 1992). These deal with the question from various perspectives, and illustrate the as yet unresolved tension between *Dignitatis Humanae* and Catholic tradition, in a way that might be seen as parallel to the work done on *Lumen Gentium* by the Australian Tracey Rowland in *Culture and the Thomist Tradition* (London, 2003). Cross's *First Things* piece is particularly useful as an overview both of the argument and of the contrast between the approach to this question taken by *Rerum Novarum* and *Centesimus Annus* (1991), though his efforts towards a solution are ultimately unpersuasive.
[31] *Op cit.*, p. 241. This is simply his restatement of the comment of Pius XII in *Ci Riesce* (1953) that "... that which does not correspond to truth or to the norm of morality objectively has no right to exist, to be spread, or to be activated."
[32] American conservative thinker Richard Weaver captured the criticality of this problem when he noted that "the enormous exertions made by the Middle Ages to preserve a common world view ... took forms incomprehensible to modern man because he does not understand what is always at stake under such circumstances." Their effort, he says, "signified a greater awareness of realities than our leaders exhibit today," when men are expected to agree upon the minutiae of daily conduct when they don't, for the most part, agree about what the world is for (*Ideas Have Consequences*, Chicago, 1948, pp. 21, 23).

[33] From the talks published as *Catholic Rural Life Objectives*.
[34] T. S. Eliot, "The idea of a Christian society", *Christianity and Culture* (New York, 1977), p. 27. On p. 17 he writes, "The problem of leading a Christian life in a non-Christian society ... is not merely the problem of a minority in a society of *individuals* holding an alien belief. It is the problem constituted by our implication in a network of institutions from which we cannot dissociate ourselves: institutions the operation of which appears no longer neutral, but non-Christian."
[35] John Paul II, *Veritatis Splendor*, 1993, 34.
[36] *Theophanous v Herald & Weekly Times Limited* (1994) 182 CLR 104.
[37] *Veritatis Splendor*, 31.
[38] Leo XIII, *Libertas*, 1888, 34.
[39] See section 41 of *Veritatis Splendor* for the centrality of obedience to God's law but its compatibility with freedom.
[40] Neither reflective liberals nor the Church accord equal rights to truth and error. John Stuart Mill (*On Liberty*, 1869) believed that in the struggle for truth, no party had a monopoly on truth and that competing ideas would produce a surer and more complete version of the truth. In its areas of authority, faith and morals, the Church of Leo and his successors foresaw the growth of the relativism and subjectivism that is commonplace today.
[41] Michael P. Fogarty, writing in the 1950s, discerns such an alignment in the values of the Christian Democrat: "The dignity of man, created in the image of God, obligates him to live in accordance with law imposed by God. Consequently he is endowed as an individual and as a member of society with rights which are inalienable. Among these rights are ... The right to freedom of expression, of information, and of communication in accordance with truth and justice." *Christian Democracy in Western Europe, 1820-1953* (South Bend, 1957, p 48).
[42] *Centisimus Annus*, 4; *Veritatis Splendor*, 32.
[43] See Eric D'Arcy, *Conscience and its Right to Freedom* (London, 1961) and more recently, Frank Brennan, *Acting on Conscience* (St Lucia, Qld, 2007).
[44] *Veritatis Splendor*, 34.
[45] Address of His Holiness Benedict XVI to the Delegates of the Academy of Moral and Political Sciences of Paris, 10 February 2007 accessed at http://www.vatican.va/holy_father/benedict_xvi/speeches/2007/february/documents/hf_ben-xvi_spe_20070210_academy-paris_en.html
[46] On participation, see *Centesimus Annus*, 35, 43, 46, 47.
[47] In similar vein see William Clifford, Ethics of Belief, *Lectures and Essays* (London, 1886 and later), which argues on ethical grounds against religious belief on insufficient evidence.
[48] Second Vatican Council, *Gaudium et Spes*, 24.
[49] *Gaudium et Spes*, 12.
[50] *Catechism of the Catholic Church* (Homebush, 1994), n1660.
[51] Universal Declaration on Human Rights, 1948, Article 16.
[52] John Paul II, *Centesimus Annus*, 39.
[53] *Centesimus Annus*, 54.
[54] James A. Brundage, *Sex, Law, and Marriage in the Middle Ages* (Aldershot, 1993).

[55] *Catechism of the Catholic Church*, 2364.
[56] Official Directory of the Catholic Church in Australia, 2006.
[57] Pope John Paul II, http://www.vatican.va/holy_father/john_paul_ii/speeches/1986/november/documents/hf_jp-ii_spe_19861126_opera-house-sydney-australia_en.html
[58] Australian Bureau of Statistics article, Australian Social Trends, Population, People in their 20s: then and now, 2006.
[59] Australian Institute of Family Studies, *Family Matters*, No. 60, Spring/Summer 2001, p. 16.
[60] Australian Institute of Health and Welfare, media release: Australia's welfare 2005 highlights.
[61] Alexandra Kirk, Tasmania passes law that recognizes same-sex relationships, *PM*, ABC Radio, Friday 29 August 2003. Same-sex couples in Tasmania will also have the same property and estate rights as married couples, bringing Tasmania into line with New South Wales, Western Australia and Victoria.
[62] Pope John Paul II, http://www.vatican.va/holy_father/john_paul_ii/speeches/1986/november/documents/hf_jp-ii_spe_19861126_opera-house-sydney-australia_en.html
[63] John XXIII, Encyclical Letter *Pacem in Terris: AAS* 55 (1963) p. 259.
[64] Second Vatican Ecumenical Council, *Gaudium et Spes,* 27: *AAS* 58 (1966), pp. 1047-48.
[65] William J. Byron, "Ten building blocks of catholic social teaching", *America Magazine*, October 1998.
[66] Second Vatican Council, *Gravissimum Educationis,* (1965) pp. 5, 6.
[67] The Universal Declaration of Human Rights (1948), Article 26.2.
[68] Byron, *ibid*.
[69] United States Conference of Catholic Bishops, *Sharing Catholic Social Teaching: Challenges and directions*, 1998 p. 5.
[70] *Catechism of the Catholic Church*, Homebush, 1994, p. 1912.
[71] Pontifical Council for Justice and Peace, *Compendium of the Social Doctrine of the Church* (Strathfield, 2005) n. 167, p. 84.
[72] J. Franklin, *Catholic Values and Australian Realities* (Ballan, 2006), p. 76.
[73] Ministerial Council on Education, Employment, Training and Youth Affairs. The Adelaide Declaration on National Goals for Schooling in the Twenty First Century, 1999.
[74] Sacred Congregation for Catholic Education, *Lay Catholics in Schools* (1982) p. 3.
[75] Genesis 1:27.
[76] J. Molony, *The Worker Question: A new historical perspective on Rerum Novarum* (North Blackburn, 1991), pp. 8-9.
[77] Australian Catholic Bishops Conference pastoral letter, *A Century of Catholic Social Teaching*, 1991.
[78] Universal Declaration of Human Rights, Art.16.
[79] *ibid*, para. 22.
[80] *Rerum Novarum*, para. 47.

[81] *ibid.*
[82] Universal Declaration, Art. 3.
[83] Department of Immigration, Multicultural & Indigenous Affairs, Report on Performance, Outcome 1 Performance Table – Effectiveness Measures, 2002-3 Annual Report, http://www.immi.gov.au/about/reports/annual/2002-03/report12.htm
[84] International Catholic Migration Commission, Strengthening Protection, p. 15 – in 1965, it was 2.3%; 1970 & 1985, 2.2%; 2000, 2.9%; 2005, 3.0%.
[85] Molony, p. 71.
[86] Ban Ki-Moon, "Welcome the dawn of the migration age", *Guardian*, 10 July 2007.
[87] M. Hogan (ed.), *Justice Now! Social Justice Statements of the Australian Catholic Bishops 1940-1966* (Sydney, 1990).
[88] M. Hogan (ed.), *Option for the Poor. Annual Social Justice Statements of the Australian Catholic Commission for Justice and Peace, 1973-1987* (Sydney, 1992), p. 173.
[89] NSW Anti-Discrimination Board, *Discrimination and Religious Conviction* (Sydney, 1984), p 227.
[90] B. Gaze & M. Jones, *Law, Liberty and Australian Democracy* (Sydney, 1990), p. 117-8.
[91] Genesis 1:27.
[92] Genesis 1:28, 29.
[93] *Laborem Exercens* (On Human Work), 4.
[94] *Populorum Progessio* (The Development of Peoples), 15-17.
[95] *Laborem Exercens*, 16.
[96] *Mater et Magistra* (Christianity and Social Progress), 74.
[97] *Gaudium et Spes* (The Church in the Modern World), 67.
[98] *Laborem Exercens*, 12, 8, 19.
[99] *Quadragesimo Anno* (The Reconstruction of the Social Order), 61.
[100] *Gaudium et Spes*, 63.
[101] *Centesimus Annus* (One Hundred Years), 43.
[102] *Laborem Exercens*, 18.
[103] *ibid.*
[104] English text available at: www.papalencyclicals.net/Leo13/l13rerum.htm
[105] *Catechism of the Catholic Church*, paragraph 2401.
[106] *Gaudium et Spes*. Promulgation by Pope Paul VI, 1965 on the Church in the Modern World 69:1. Available at www.ewtn.com/library/COUNCILS/v2modwor.htm
[107] See *Catechism of the Catholic Church*, paragraphs 1929 through 1942.
[108] Full text of the UN Declaration of Human Rights available at: www.un.org/Overview/rights.html
[109] J. Ryan, *A Living Wage* (London, 1906).
[110] R. Ederer, *Economics As If God Mattered: A Century of Papal Teaching* (South Bend, 1995).

[111] C. Panico, *Interest and Profit in the Theories of Value and Distribution* (Houndsmills, UK), 1988.
[112] *Rerum Novarum*, n.3 of online version.
[113] M. Pusey, *The Experience of Middle Australia* (Cambridge, UK, 2003).
[114] T. Woods, The unanswered questions of the just wage. *Catholic Social Teaching and the Market Economy*, ed. P. Booth (London, 2007).
[115] M. Novak, *Freedom with Justice* (New York, 1984).
[116] F. Harrison, *The Power in the Land* (New York, 1983).
[117] J.T. Rogers, *Six Centuries of Work and Wages* (London, 1884).
[118] O. Langholm, *Economics in the Medieval Schools: Wealth, Exchange, Value, Money and Usury According to the Paris Theological Tradition* (New York, 1992).
[119] Bishop Manning, 28 June 2006, address at Rooty Hill RSL Club, Diocesan Forum on WorkChoices.
[120] B. Webb & S. Webb, *The History of Trade Unionism* (London, 1894); S. Webb, *Industrial Democracy* (London, 1897).
[121] Quoted in M. Kirby and B. Creighton, The law of conciliation and arbitration, *The New Province for Law and Order: 100 years of Australian industrial conciliation and arbitration,* eds. J. Isaac and S. Macintyre (Melbourne, 2004), p. 102.
[122] Pope Paul VI, *Populorum Progressio* (London, 1967) par. 59.
[123] *Rerum Novarum*, par 49.
[124] ibid, par 50.
[125] See, for example, John Paul II, *Laborem Exercens*, par 20: http://www.vatican.va/edocs/ENG0217/__PL.HTM
[126] B. Duncan, *The Church's Social Teaching: From Rerum Novarum to 1931* (Blackburn, Vic., 1991), p. 23.
[127] Quoted in J.G. Murtagh, *Australia – the Catholic Chapter* (Melbourne, 1969), p. 127.
[128] ibid, p. 129.
[129] See M. Rimmer, Unions and arbitration, in Isaac and Macintyre, op. cit., p. 279.
[130] B. Dabscheck, A new province for law and order: The Australian experiment with industrial tribunals, in J. Niland, R. Lansbury and C. Verevis, (eds.), *The Future of Industrial Relations* (Thousand Oaks, 1994), p. 64.
[131] *Mater et Magistra*, http://www.vatican.va/holy_father/john_xxiii/encyclicals/documents/hf_j-xxiii_enc_15051961_mater_en.html, par. 97
[132] ibid, par 103.
[133] See ILO website for text of "Fundamental Conventions" on the right to organise and collective bargaining: http://www.ilo.org/ilolex/english/subjectE.htm#s01
[134] Address to workers at the Transfield factory, Parramatta, 26 November 1986, quoted in ACCER, Briefing Paper No. 1 on the Commonwealth Government's Proposals to Reform Workplace Relations in Australia, p. 22.
[135] Benedict XVI, *On Christian Love* (Strathfield, 2006), par. 16.

[136] I would like to express my appreciation and gratitude to James Franklin and Damian Grace for their guidance and valuable comments in the preparation of this work.
[137] Leo XIII, 1891, *Rerum Novarum*, www.vatican.va/holy_father/leo_xiii/encyclicals/documents/hf_l-xiii_enc_15051891_rerum-novarum_en.html.
[138] This is affirmed in the United Nations Universal Declaration of Human Rights, 1948, www.un.org/overview/rights.html
[139] *Rerum Novarum,* 50.
[140] Cited in E. Freidson, *Professionalism: The Third Logic,* University of Chicago Press, Chicago, 2001, p. 11.
[141] *Rerum Novarum,* 33.
[142] J. Rawls, *A Theory of Justice: Revised Edition* Belknap Press, Cambridge, Mass., 1999, pp. 3-10.
[143] *Rerum Novarum,* 58.
[144] Koehn, D., *The Ground of Professional Ethics,* Routledge, London, 1994, p. 179. This is a recurring theme throughout Koehn's book.
[145] See M. Coady and S. Bloch (eds), *Codes of Ethics and the Professions* (Carlton South, 1996), pp. 4-7; and J. Kultgen, *Ethics and Professionalism* (Philadelphia, 1988), Chapter 7.
[146] Freidson, p. 198.
[147] For further information and discussion about the issues of monopoly, credentialism and competition with respect to the professions, see the Australian Competition and Consumer Commission (ACCC) website, www.accc.gov.au/content/index.phtml/itemId/6193/fromItemId/3669 (22 August 2007)
[148] Freidson, Chapter 10.
[149] An individual does not need to be a member of the association that is negotiating on their behalf.
[150] For an explanation of the form and content of codes of ethics, see D. Grace and S. Cohen, *Business Ethics: Problems and Cases*, Third Edition, Oxford University Press, South Melbourne, 2005, Chapter 10.
[151] M. Coady, 'The moral domain of professionals', in Coady & Bloch, Chapter 2.
[152] Charles, R, *An Introduction to Catholic Social Teaching*, Family Publications, Oxford, 1999, p. 15
[153] *Rerum Novarum*, 1891, section 50.
[154] Charles, 1999, p. 15
[155] *Gaudium et Spes*, 1965, 25.
[156] *Libertatis Conscientia* (1986), Congregation for the Doctrine of the Faith, Instruction, http://www.vatican.va/roman_curia/congregations/cfaith/documents/rc_con_cfaith_doc_19860322_freedom-liberation_en.html
[157] Charles, 1999, p. 35.
[158] *Quadragesimo Anno*, 1931, 79.
[159] Charles, 1999, p. 36.
[160] *Libertatis Conscientia*, 1986, 73.
[161] Charles, 1999, p. 36.

[162] Charles, R, *Christian Witness and Teaching: The Catholic Tradition from Genesis to Centesimus Annus*, Vol. 1, From Biblical Times to the Late Nineteenth Century, Gracewing, Herefordshire, 1998, p. 64.
[163] Pontifical Council for Justice and Peace, *Compendium of the Social Doctrine of the Church,* Burns and Oates, (London, 2004), 219, 226-28, 254.
[164] *Compendium,* 2004, 155.
[165] *Centesimus Annus*, 1991, 48.

INDEX

Aborginal Australians 18, 39, 101, 124
Abortion 35, 41
Aquinas 20-1, 99, 101
Aristotle 4, 94-5
Assembly, right of 84-6
Assistance from society, right to 117-22
Association, right of 81-4
Association by industries and professionals, right to 111-5

Benedict XVI 47, 110
Bonaventure, St 104
Briefs, G 23-4
Byron,W 57, 59

Canute 6
Capital punishment 16
Catechesi tradendae 29
Cathechism of the Catholic Church 52-3, 95
Catholic Commission for Justice and Peace 83
Centesimus annus 64, 67, 121
Chesterton, GK 99
Coady T 115
Collective bargaining, right to 105-10
Communism 3, 83
Compendium of the Social Doctrine of the Church 105, 120
Conscience 21-2

Decatur, S 21
Dignitatis humanae 22

Ederer, R 100
Education 30, 57-62
Eliot, TS 19, 24
Equal protection, right to 39-44

Fahey, D 21
Family 52, 55, 77, 118
Franklin J 60
Freedom, see liberty
Freedom of expression, right to 45-9
Freedom of the press 64-5
Freidson E 113-4

Galileo 45
Gaudium et spes 74, 83, 117
Gilmore, M 93
Gravissimum educationis 58

Harrison F 102
Harvester case 12
Hayek, F 4, 6
Health, rights to 18
Helsinki Accords 1
Hoffman, RJS 21

Immigrants 43, 72-3, 79-80
International Labour Organization 109

Jesus 15, 29, 45-6, 97
John XXIII 74, 89, 109
John Paul II 8, 15, 29, 35, 45-6, 54-5, 64, 67, 74, 87, 89, 103, 109, 121
Judt, T 1

King, ML 17
Koehn D 113

Laborem exercens 87
Labour market 8-9, 12
Laissez faire capitalism 3, 97, 103, 108
Law and ethics 7-8, 33-4, 39, 42
Lay Catholics in Schools 61
Leo XIII, see Rerum novarum
Libertatis conscientia 118
Liberty, religious 21, 28
Liberty, right to personal 33-7
Life, right to 15-18, 75, 99
Livelihood, right to 75-80

Mao 11
Manning K 105
Mannix, D 21
Maritain, J. 21
Markets 7, 10, 100, 102-4, 110
Marriage 52-6
Marx, K 4
Mater et magistra 109
McIntyre, A 94
Migration, right to 72, 78-80
Mill, JS 96
Mit brennender Sorge 42, 46
Moran, P 82, 108

Nationality, right to 69-74
Natural law ethics 2, 20, 42, 95, 99, 119
Nazism 41-2, 46

Ownership, right to 93-97

Panico, C 101
Participation in society, right to 63, 77
Paul VI 74, 87, 106
Petition, right to 63-7
Pius XI 42, 46, 82, 89
Populorum progressio 106
Professional associations 112-5

Quadragesimo anno 82, 118

Rawls J 112
Relativism 1
Religion, right to 19-25, 84-5
Religious formation, right to 27-31
Religious vocation 27, 53, 55-6
Rerum novarum 3, 11-12, 16, 19-20, 46, 64, 76, 79, 81-2, 93-5, 96, 99-101, 104-7, 111-2
Ryan, J 99
Roosevelt T 58

Safety 7, 17
Second Vatican Council 22, 28, 58, 83, 89
Self-organisation 5-7
Slavery 7, 50
Smith, A. 4
Social justice 4, 6, 13, 83
Socialism 3
Solidarity 71-2, 96, 106, 119
Soviet Union 1
Srebrenica 15
State intervention 9, 11-12, 60, 90, 121
State of life, right to choose 51-6
Subsidiarity 10, 67, 118-9

Trade unions 82, 103, 105-8

UN International Covenant on Civil
and Political Rights 64-6
Universal Declaration of Human
Rights 21, 45, 51-2, 57, 60, 76, 78,
87, 97, 99
Usury 100-1

Veritatis splendor 46, 103
Voltaire 47

Wage, right to minimum 12, 77, 89,
99-104
Webb B 105
Weber, M 5
Weigel, G 35
Woods T 102
Work, right to 87-91

Life to the Full